today and all the days of your life

Writers and Editors:

Jeanne Martin

Gail McDonough

Susan Hannibal

Susan Edwards

K. Diane Daly

Dixie Meyer

Videographer:

Chuck Neff
Stepstone Productions, Inc.

Archdiocese of Saint Louis and Liguori Publications

A PROGRAM OF MARRIAGE PREPARATION

Imprimi Potest:
Richard Thibodeau, C.Ss.R.
The Redemptorists, Denver Province

Imprimatur:
Most Reverend Timothy M. Dolan, V.G.
Auxiliary Bishop of Saint Louis

Today and All the Days of Your Life, as a complete program, includes an eight segment video series, the Couple Workbook and a Facilitator Guide.

© 2002, Archdiocese of Saint Louis
ISBN 0-7648-1278-5
Printed in the United States of America
08 07 06 05   5 4 3 2

Published by Liguori Publications
One Liguori Drive
Liguori, Missouri 63057-9999
1-800-325-9521
www.liguori.org

In agreement withthe Office of Laity & Family Life
Archdiocese of Saint Louis
20 Archbishop May Drive
Saint Louis, Missouri 63119
314.792.7170
www.stlcatholics.org

Today and All the Days of Your Life
is a complete program.

The video series and Couple Workbook
are complementary to each other.

The videos are not to be used
without the Couple Workbook.

The workbook is not to be used
without the videos.

The Faciliatator Guide is a necessary
component because each chapter
builds upon the previous chapter.

PLEASE use this program as intended.

Archdiocese of Saint Louis and Liguori Publications

A PROGRAM OF MARRIAGE PREPARATION

Publishers Preface

Today and All the Days of Your Life is truly a team effort of the staff of the Archdiocese of Saint Louis' Office of Laity & Family Life. It took years, countless hours and a great deal of financial support, to complete. We are grateful to be generously supported year after year by grants from the annual Archdiocesan Development Appeal. While being proud of this program, we know without a doubt that "God is in the details." (Mies van der Rohe)

Introducing the Office of Laity & Family Life Staff who are the Writers and Editors:

Jeanne Martin-married to Tom for 32 years, mother of three adult daughters and grandmother of three. As a Consultant to the office, with vast experience in marriage preparation programs, she wrote the first draft of the Couple Workbook. She has a Master of Arts in Religious Studies and previously worked as a high school Theology teacher and in parish adult religious education. Jeanne is the author of *Facing Cancer with God's Help*, (Liguori Publications 9/01). Jeanne ended her courageous battle with cancer by entering into eternal life on February 8, 2004.

Susan Hannibal-married to Kurt for five years (newly engaged when we began!). She is the Coordinator of Marriage Preparation and is creator of the theme for this program. It was her original concept to weave the design around the promises and vows to help couples better understand the commitment they were making on their wedding day. Her daily experiences talking to and scheduling classes for the engaged, together with her skills in the art of language were invaluable.

Gail McDonough-married to Mike for 40 years, mother of one son and three daughters, all of whom are adults. She is the grandmother of five. Gail is the Coordinator of Marriage Program Development. In the role of Project Manager for this program, she researched, scheduled, wrote and edited, pushed, prodded, cajoled and inspired us. Her dedication and perseverance were unwavering during the videotaping and as she developed the necessary skills to enable us to self-publish this book.

K. Diane Daly-married to Tom for 37 years, mother of four adult children and grandmother of a baby boy. As Coordinator of the Archdiocesan Department of Natural Family Planning, Diane is a registered nurse who has worked in this field for 26 years and is nationally recognized for her contributions. She is a pioneer in the Creighton Model Fertility Care System, a system used to achieve or avoid pregnancy naturally and used for women's health care through NaProTechnology.

Dixie Meyer-married to Samuel for five years. She is the Marriage and Family Assistant for the office and is currently working on her Master's in Marriage and Family Counseling. Her attention to detail was meticulous as she gathered references, became a wordsmith extraordinaire, and compiled and disseminated the materials necessary for the piloting of the program.

Susan Edwards-married to Robert for 39 years, mother of two adult daughters, and grandmother of two baby girls. She is the Executive Director of the Office of Laity & Family Life, holds a Masters degree in Pastoral Studies and is a Licensed Clinical Social Worker. Susan was previously a psychotherapist in private practice and helped to provide the Archdiocesan umbrella under which *Today and All the Days of Your Life* was created.

Acknowledgements

Today and All the Days of Your Life would not have been possible without the help of literally hundreds of people. The Office of Laity & Family Life is not able to thank all of them personally, but we are grateful to our "marriage experts" who worked on this program and drew upon their 1000 plus years of marital experience. Throughout this process we agonized over the question "What can we do to help couples keep the promises and vows they make on their wedding day?"

The inspiration for this program came from a marriage preparation team in the Archdiocese of Saint Louis. This team included Deacon Bill & Mary Gearon, Joseph & Pat Hagele, John & Eleanore Heithaus, Rich & Maureen Keys, Gail & Mike McDonough, Kristie & Andy Lenzen and Jim & Susan Odom. Our heartfelt gratitude is extended to these couples for their work in this ministry.

The stories of our Saint Louis couples were woven masterfully together by Chuck Neff of Stepstone Productions, Inc. and his wonderful staff, which includes Jennifer Roller, Megan Matheny, Jeff Wilmes, R.T. Radanovic, Zlatko Cosic and Mike Burke. Voiceovers were graciously performed by Maria Rodgers O'Rourke, former Director of the Office of Laity & Family Life and Chuck Neff. Additionally, Chuck Neff crafted the scripts for each video segment.

Archbishop Justin Rigali, Auxiliary Bishop Timothy Dolan (now Archbishop of Milwaukee, Wisconsin) and Chancellor, Monsignor Richard Stika, supported us throughout this project. Monsignor Ted Wojcicki, Vicar for Pastoral Planning, advised us - often in late night emails. We also thank Rev. Jeff Vomund and Rev. Eugene Morris who appear in our videos and counseled us on content.

The people who share some of their stories on the videos are an inspiration to engaged couples everywhere. We thank:

Joseph & Missy Bradlo	Andy & Kristie Lenzen
Robert & Susan Edwards	Bob & Jenni Naville
Juan Escarfuller & Dalmys Sanchez	Steve & Pat Notestine
K. Diane Daly	Jim & Susan Odom
Deacon Bill & Mary Gearon	Jeff & Jeanne Stoll
Kurt & Susan Hannibal	Dan & Paula Stoverink
Deacon Phil & Mary Hengen	Tim & Sherry Wichmer
Jim & Teresa Kahre	Norman & Linda Williams
Joe & Beth Londino, M.D.	

We appreciate all of our Archdiocesan class facilitators, deacons, priests and those who offer other programs of marriage preparation who came together in focus groups to give advice and feedback in the early days of video production and workbook creation. *Today and All the Days of Your Life* was molded and shaped by the carefully completed evaluations of facilitators who piloted our program one-on-one, in small and large classes and in a one-day format. Although they are too numerous to mention by name, we give thanks for their advice and suggestions.

Thanks also to our classroom participants appearing on the video. They include Dalmys Sanchez and Juan Escarfuller; Michelle Surmeier and Matthew Mentel; Tuan and Thuong Nguyen; Olivia and Christopher Pieknik; Jessica Hardebeck and Matt Schellman; Keith Samuels and Barb Buscher and all of the engaged couples who appeared in our videos and are too numerous to mention. Over 1200 couples participated in the pilot sessions of this program. The value of their input through evaluations and other feedback can never be measured.

Suggestions and support for "Stewardship and Your Finances" came from Mr. Frank Cognata, Chief Development Officer and Monsignor Ted Wojcicki, Vicar for Pastoral Planning for the Archdiocese of Saint Louis. Victoria A. Jacobson, President of the Foundation for Credit Education, graciously gave permission for the use of their *Newlyweds' Guide to Money Management*.

We would like to thank PAIRS, International for providing materials and inspiration for the communication segment of this program, especially Drs. Lori and Morris Gordon, founders.

We are grateful to all couples who allowed us to use their wedding videos to open each segment; especially Joseph & Melissa Bradlo, Andrea & Fred Douglas and Tuan & Thuong Nguyen.

Last, but not least, a very special thanks to the rest of the staff of the Office of Laity & Family Life who supported and participated in the process from beginning to end, including: Rose Bley, Sarah Hoenninger, Kathleen Jamboretz, Kristie Lenzen, Dwight Mazanec, Jo Ann Owings, Greg Rohde and Carol Tempel.

Gail McDonough
Coordinator, Marriage Program Development
Project Manager for *Today and All the Days of Your Life*
and The Development Team

Table of Contents

Chapter 1:

SACRAMENT OF
MATRIMONY

I TAKE YOU TO
BE MY SPOUSE

Sacrament of Marriage - The Covenant of a man and a woman and God, joined in a commitment to share life and love in the vocation of marriage. The couple receives grace from the Sacrament to love each other with the love of Christ. This special love of the couple becomes a sign of Jesus' love in the world.

" The vocation to marriage is written in the very nature of man and woman as they came from the hand of the Creator."

Catechism of the Catholic Church #1603

*W*hen Tom and I were married, I had no clear understanding of the Sacrament of Matrimony. I thought we were going to church to "get" the sacrament - that it was a one day event. Then, it was just Tom and me, a dream for a house, three or four children, a dog and the promise of certain happiness and joy each day of our marriage. Our relationship was private and no one should care what kind of marriage we had except the two of us. It took a few years for me to realize that something special happened on our wedding day that had the potential to affect the strength and quality of our everyday relationship.

I soon realized that daily happiness and joy was difficult to sustain in the face of such things as the stress of becoming parents, trying to balance in-law visits and holiday celebrations, keeping the romance alive when we were busy changing diapers and building a career, forgiving each other for saying the wrong thing at the wrong time, etc.

A PERSONAL STORY

by Jeanne M.

As we achieved a clearer understanding of what we GAVE each other on our wedding day - the Sacrament of Marriage - and that God is our partner in our marriage and not just an uninvolved bystander, everything seemed to change. The sacrament was not something we received one time. It was something we were affirming in the day-to-day decisions of trying to love each other in the face of ordinary difficulties (and some extraordinary ones).

Through our sacrament, I had the grace (God's presence) to forgive Tom when I just could not do it on my own. God was there in our lives in a very special and unique way to help us make the decision to love one another and allow our relationship to be more important than the issue with which we were struggling. With the love of Jesus as our model, we could handle anything. Not only were we being transformed as individuals, but our relationship as a married couple was reflecting this divine love to our family, friends, coworkers, neighbors and all the people of the Church.

How we love each other, sacrifice for one another, forgive each other and respect each other, makes a difference to those around us. In this Sacrament of Matrimony we have the potential to "put flesh on God," allowing others to experience Jesus' love by witnessing our sacramental love. When we do it right, people will look at us and begin to understand how much God loves them. How we heal our hurts, love unconditionally and show unity, indicates to others God's unconditional love, that is, God's faithful love and commitment to each of us.

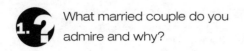 What married couple do you admire and why?

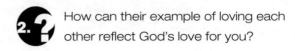 How can their example of loving each other reflect God's love for you?

 Name one thing you want people to see in your marriage commitment.

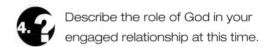 Describe the role of God in your engaged relationship at this time.

 Describe how you plan to make God a part of your marriage.

Christ dwells with them [husbands and wives], gives them the strength to take up their crosses and so follow him, to rise again after they have fallen, to forgive one another, to bear one another's burdens, to "be subject to one another out of reverence for Christ," (Eph 5:21; cf. Gal 6:2) and to love one another with supernatural, tender, and fruitful love.

Catechism of the Catholic Church #1642

6. How do you feel when you hear that the success of your marriage is important to the church?

☑ Check all that apply.

_____ eager to create a strong marriage   _____ makes me reconsider a church wedding
_____ open to the challenge   _____ makes me doubt we are up to it
_____ puzzled   _____ frightened

 7. What is the most appealing thing to you about being so important to the Church?

☑ Check all that apply.

_____ knowing that there are marriage enrichment programs that we can attend
_____ having a community in which we can share our celebrations and our struggles
_____ being encouraged to be more committed to working on problem areas
_____ our family is connected with a church family
_____ we are not alone in this
_____ other _____

8. Have you asked for God's help to make this commitment? Are you willing to put your spouse first in your married relationship? Are you willing to continuously invite God to be a partner in your marriage?

Father Eugene Morris said...

"It is this public relationship of mutual support that is celebrated in your marriage - in its liturgical, communal reality. This is the importance of coming to the Church, not only to stand before God and confirm the reality of your Christ-centered and Christ-rooted love, but also to allow the Church to publicly affirm Her commitment to you."

Deacon Bill Gearon used clay models to visualize the distinction between a contract marriage and a covenant marriage. In a covenant marriage, God shapes us, making one heart where there were two. It is a partnership. The husband, wife and God **together** form a covenant that is **exclusive, permanent, unconditional and faithful.**

Contract Marriage vs Covenant Marriage

- involves man & woman	- involves man, woman and God
- law based	- love based
- can be legally dissolved	- permanent
- conditional on fulfillment of contract	- unconditional
- concerns rights and duties of the individuals	- concerns the well-being of the couple who are united uniquely through the love of Christ

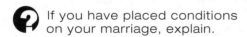 **Be sure to discuss your answers to these questions this week.**

 9. Do you privately believe there are "deal-breakers" in your marriage? For example,

infertility	sexual dysfunction	debilitating illness
substance abuse	extra-marital affair	job change requiring relocating
addictions	multiple births	over-spending or being stingy with money
disabled child	decrease in income	spouse leaves the Catholic faith

 If you have placed conditions on your marriage, explain.

If such a situation occurs in your marriage, would you be willing to seek professional assistance? If not, why not?

Living your life as a Christian married couple means you will also share in the cross of Christ. When Jesus tells us to love as he has loved, it means there will be suffering in our relationships. When we have to lay down our life, our way of thinking and doing things, for the good of the relationship, we die to ourselves and our self-centeredness. As we do this, we rise, as Jesus did, to a new life. When married couples embrace their differences and embrace change, then in the end it is the marriage ... the two of you ... who grow. It is the marriage that wins.

 Give an example of putting aside what you wanted in order to strengthen your relationship. How did you feel about making this sacrifice and the decision to love?

 Give an example of when your fiancé made a personal sacrifice in order to strengthen your relationship. How did this decision to love make you feel?

 How do you experience or encounter God's love through your fiancé? Be specific. (e.g. in acceptance, forgiveness, gentleness, honesty, depth, surprises ...)

 "Yet, if we love **one another,** God remains in us, and his love is brought to perfection in us."

1 Jn. 4:12

Your passionate love for one another reflects to the world how much God loves each of us. You are a visible sign of God's love!

Chapter 2:
FAMILY OF ORIGIN

I TAKE YOU

Your **Family of Origin** is the family you grew up in or the persons who raised you. You may have been raised by a single-parent or two parents, a grandparent or caretaker. Your family of origin also includes any children raised along with you. These are the people who influenced your values, established your expectations and shaped your attitudes about life. These people were your role models for marriage, work and relationships. Just as you were formed by your own family of origin, so too was your fiancé. Over the years these influences have developed into different personal habits, attitudes, ways of thinking, values and behaviors for each of you.

It is very important for you to be aware of the thoughts, feelings and attitudes you bring into your marriage. In the video, Kristie and Andy Lenzen showed you their suitcases which contained both the good and the troublesome that they unknowingly brought into their marriage. Some items in their suitcases helped them to form a happy home, some caused problems and unhappiness. At times your patterns of behavior or style of living may irritate your spouse. It is important to remember that when you marry, and pledge: "I take you ..." to be my husband or wife, you say you will accept and love your spouse as they are, the good and the bad, **with no expectation of changing them or their behavior.**

That does not mean you will not **change** or **grow** as you join your lives day by day. It means that each person is **responsible** for their **own change.** You **cannot change** another person, **only yourself**. You **can,** however, **communicate** about how you **feel** and allow your spouse the **freedom** to take that into **consideration, without expectations.**

your suitcase

 1. What's in your suitcase?

Choose and describe two things that were important in your family of origin.

work ethic	sports
standard of living	religion
where to live	education
type of car	buying what you want
politics	roles of husband/wife
entertainment choices	neatness
showing affection	vacations
saving money	TV habits
health maintenance choices	family togetherness
expressing feelings	how to spend a Saturday

Kristie said...

"Sometimes you want things the way you want things - especially if you both have strong personalities, **(big sticks!)** but the important thing is to 'get below' those kinds of things to what we want together, which is a good marriage relationship."

 What is in your suitcase that you are happy about and proud to bring into your marriage?

 Name some things in your suitcase that are difficult for you and may become problem areas in your marriage.

 Dr. Gary Smalley, a well known author, states that happy families have these six things in common.(1)

 Rate these qualities for your Family of Origin.

	Very Good	Good	Poor	Not at all
Appreciate each other				
Spend time together				
Good communication				
Strong sense of commitment to family unit				
Deeply felt religious beliefs				
Ability to deal with crisis positively				

Choose one to discuss with your fiancé.

 What are some similarities in your background and your fiancé's background?

 What are some important differences?

holiday preferences

 7. Take Christmas as an example:
What is the one Christmas tradition you must have to make the holidays complete?

 8. How will you spend the Christmas holidays while trying to accommodate the wishes of your respective families?

 9. For Christmas, do you prefer...

_____ a fat Christmas tree	OR	_____ a Charlie Brown tree
_____ small nativity scene for table	OR	_____ large nativity scene as focal point
_____ live tree	OR	_____ artificial tree
_____ white lights	OR	_____ colored lights
_____ lots of decorations	OR	_____ minimal decorations
_____ midnight Mass	OR	_____ morning Mass
_____ formal dinner	OR	_____ casual buffet
_____ American classic food	OR	_____ ethnic traditional food
_____ big budget for gifts	OR	_____ small budget for gifts

HERE'S A TIP | FIND CREATIVE WAYS TO DEAL WITH YOUR **FAMILY OF ORIGIN** DIFFERENCES.

- try talking about tough issues only after anger has subsided
- pray together and apart - develop a relationship with God
- attend marriage enrichment days to learn new communication skills
- attend marriage counseling
- be active in your church community

in-laws

 10. List several things you like about your fiancé's family.

 11. What don't you like about your fiancé's family?

 12. Are you comfortable with your future in-laws? Why or why not?

 13. Describe the kind of relationship you would like to have with your family and your spouse's family?

How often would you see them?

Would you mind if they drop in without calling first?

Would you want to live near them?

Would you give them keys to your house?

Would you go on vacation with them?

 14. Do you feel supported by your future spouse, in terms of your values and opinions, when you are with your fiancé's parents and siblings? If not, explain.

 15. Are you comfortable with the type and quality of relationship your fiancé has with his/her parents? Is it just right, too close, not close enough? Explain.

> ❝ Therefore a man leaves his father and his mother and cleaves to his wife, and they become one flesh. ❞ (Gen 2:24) The Lord himself shows that this signifies an unbreakable union of their two lives by recalling what the plan of the Creator had been 'in the beginning': ❝ So they are no longer two, but one flesh. ❞ (Mt 19:6)
>
> *Catechism of the Catholic Church #1605*

personality traits

Put your initials next to the traits you see in yourself; put your fiancé's initials next to his/her traits.

____Easy-going	____Quick to anger	____Diligent	____Kind
____Loyal	____Considerate	____Religious	____Stubborn
____Sentimental	____Mean streak	____Observant	____Leader
____Creative	____Introverted	____Extroverted	____Quiet
____Impulsive	____Family centered	____Cautious	____Patient
____Talkative	____Judgmental	____Fair	____Liberal
____Practical	____Conservative	____Innovative	____Peaceful
____Gentle	____Legalistic	____Moody	____Selfish
____Direct	____Control Freak	____Organized	____Joyful
____Honest	____Happy-go-lucky	____Playful	____Generous
____Stingy	____Depressive	____Well-liked	____Strong
____Flexible	____Emotional	____Loner	____Sad
____Serious	____Dishonest	____Prejudiced	____Trust-worthy

 Next to your fiancé's traits, check those that attracted you to him/her.

 And circle those that concern you.

 Does your fiancé have some behavior you hope will change after you are married? If so, what is it? What will you do if there is no change? Can you live with it as it is?

When you say the vow "I Take You…"

What you are promising is that "I take you … as you really are: with the personality you have, the spirituality you have, with the ideas, values and ways of being that you developed within your family of origin. I take you with all your good qualities and those that sometimes irritate me and I am willing to work through the years to make our marriage truly a joy, with God's help."

roles and expectations

Complete these questions about some everyday, ordinary choices you will make in your marriage.

17. Indicate who should be responsible for various chores.

_____yard work   _____cleaning the bathroom   _____dusting/vacuuming

_____washing clothes   _____cooking   _____doing dishes

_____taking out the garbage   _____grocery shopping   _____car maintenance

18. Who will pay the bills? _____

What is the "right" way to put socks away? _____

Will you recycle cans/plastic? _____

Which way should you put on the toilet paper roll? _____

What is your preferred time to wake up? _____   to go to bed? _____

19. In what types of stores will you shop (i.e. discount, family department store, high end retail, speciality shops, etc.)?

> "Love is patient, love is kind. It is not jealous, [love] is not pompous, it is not inflated, it is not rude, it does not seek its own interests, it is not quick-tempered, it does not brood over injury, it does not rejoice over wrongdoing but rejoices with the truth. It bears all things, believes all things, hopes all things, endures all things."
>
> 1 Cor. 13:4-7

Finding God in the Ordinary...

The Sacrament of Marriage calls us to love our spouse as Christ loves us. This sounds so impossible and overwhelming. But the reality is that _it is in the ordinary, everyday, nitty-gritty circumstances of our lives that we make God real to one another._ The attitude we bring to taking out the garbage or scrubbing the bathroom can send a strong message that "I'm happy to do this for us." This is love in action - a transforming kind of love. We become a couple who mirrors God's love by how we live and love in the ordinary.

taking the time to build your marriage

Balancing time with your spouse along with job requirements and children/family needs was cited as one of the most problematic areas in the first five years of marriage.(2) After the rush of the wedding subsides, as couples begin to create a routine for everyday life, it is important to make time for one another. Building a married relationship requires time alone for just the two of you. It becomes too easy to move from a stage of romance to one of disillusionment when couples are distracted from focusing on one another because of countless requirements on their time. Time is so precious and where we spend our time is where we place our hearts.

 How do you expect to spend your leisure time?

- List activities you would do without your spouse.

- List activities you and your spouse would do together.

- List activities you and your spouse would share with friends.

 Describe a normal weekend after you are married.

 How often do you plan to spend time with your friends that will exclude your spouse? How do you think your spouse will feel about this?

Weekly _____   Monthly _____

Twice a month _____   Other_____

 Are you comfortable with all of your fiancé's friends? If not, have you discussed this with your fiancé?

 Do you have any concerns about the activities your fiancé participates in without you?

for Catholic couples

 How have you been influenced by God in your past?
☑ Check all that apply.

___ God/faith were important in my family of origin experiences.

___ I learned about God in school.

___ My faith has had a positive influence in shaping my values and morals.

___ I've come to relate to God/Jesus in a personal way.

___ I feel living my Christian faith and practicing my Catholic religion is important.

 What religious traditions or customs would you like to bring to your marriage? (e.g. prayers before meals, holding hands at Mass during the Our Father, Midnight Mass at Christmas, bedtime prayers together, etc.)

 Do you expect to go to Mass together each week?

 Do you believe you can respect and support your spouse's personal faith and religious practices?

 Do you believe your spouse will respect and support your personal faith and religious practices?

for interreligious couples

Catholics create interreligious marriages when their spouses are of another Christian denomination or a non-Christian faith. When two people from different faith backgrounds join their lives in marriage, it takes some thought and planning to handle differences so that each feels affirmed and respected in their own faith backgrounds.

Respect your differences, but celebrate your shared beliefs. The wedding ceremony between a Catholic and a person of a different faith often does not include the Liturgy of the Eucharist with reception of Holy Communion out of respect for the spouse, their family members and friends who are unable to receive Communion. Your priest or deacon can help you plan your ceremony to make it a meaningful and beautiful celebration of unity.

 How have you been influenced by God in your past?
✔ Check all that apply.

___ God/faith were important in my family of origin experiences.

___ I learned about God in religious/Sunday school.

___ My faith has had a positive influence in shaping my values and morals.

___ I've come to relate to God/Jesus in a personal way.

___ I feel living my faith and practicing my religion is important.

 Do you believe you can respect and support your spouse's personal faith and religious practices?

 Do you believe your spouse will respect and support your personal faith and religious practices? If not, why not?

HERE'S A TIP

Some suggestions from couples in interreligious marriages:

- be sensitive to one another
- take time to learn about one another's religious beliefs and practices
- attend one another's worship services
- do not stop practicing your own faith in order to keep peace as this may result in resentment

33. Will you attend each other's worship services?

 34. What religious traditions or customs would you like to bring to your marriage?

 35. What are some beliefs about God or some worship practices your two religions have in common?

 36. What are the main differences?

 37. When being married in the Catholic Church, the Catholic spouse promises to raise your children in the Catholic faith. Will this pose a problem for your marriage?

According to *Ministry to Interchurch Marriages,* a study done by the Center for Marriage and Family at Creighton University, "a significant predictor of marital stability is participation in joint religious activities ..."(3)

 38. Is there something you are afraid to discuss regarding your different religious beliefs? If so, what is it? (i.e., something you fear your future spouse may not understand or respect.)

 39. Are you willing to study your fiancé's beliefs in order to grow more deeply together in faith and in understanding of one another? What are some ways you can do this?

You are invited...

to learn about the Catholic faith

Most Catholic parishes offer a process of Christian

initiation called the Rite of Christian Initiation of Adults.

(RCIA). The process invites those attending to

explore, deepen and strengthen their faith and their

relationship with God while learning about the

beliefs and practices of the Catholic faith.

Participants are non-Catholics interested in

understanding Catholic beliefs, as well as those

who desire to become Catholic. Occasionally

Catholics who want to more fully understand

their faith join RCIA. Often a Catholic spouse,

fiancé or friend accompanies their non-Catholic

partner on this journey of faith. Call your local parish

for information about the RCIA program.

PRAYER

Lord, we thank you for those in our family of origin and all others who have loved us, taught us and helped make us who we are today. We are ready to join our lives now with someone we love and create a new family. We thank you for giving us a new Life in You. We ask daily for the grace to love and accept one another fully, and to be a reflection of your Light in us.

Amen.

You both arrived with your own suitcases. Together you must pack a bag for your marriage journey.

FAMILY OF ORIGIN

Chapter 3: ROMANCE, DISILLUSIONMENT & JOY

IN GOOD TIMES
AND IN BAD

You have been listening to the couples in the video segments relate their
stories of love and marriage. The Hengens, Gearons, Odoms and Lenzens
have all shared the special romantic way they met, **"fell in love"** and
decided to get married. But their stories do not end here. In this video in
particular, you heard about how the honeymoon ended and **disillusionment**
set in. Many couples in today's society are unprepared for the natural changes
occurring in their relationship. As a result, many young couples may call it
quits as soon as disillusionment sets in.

In marriage preparation, it is very important to understand the natural
cycle of **Romance, Disillusionment and Joy** that will recur throughout
married life. By understanding this cycle, couples realize that they are capable
of working through the difficult times to then welcome joy. Husbands and

wives CAN create **romance** and keep it alive in their marriages, and the Sacrament of Marriage provides couples with the grace needed to handle struggles. All relationships are affected by similar three part cycles, even those between co-workers, classmates, neighbors, family members and friends.

Love relationships begin with a romance phase. This is marked by close, tender feelings. During this time it is so easy to do things for the other person and to put their wants and needs before yours. You are easily affectionate and you like being with the other person. You can readily overlook your spouse's faults and concentrate on their goodness.

Disillusionment sets in when you get so caught up in the daily grind that life becomes routine. The glamour fades and you begin to focus more on faults and less on goodness. You begin to take each other for granted and the excitement and wonder of the relationship seems to disappear. Problems and difficult times have the potential to cause resentment, disagreements and hurts. The question often arises: "Is this all there is?"

This is my commandment:
" Love one another
as I love you."

John 15:12

Now the work begins. This Sacrament calls you to learn unconditional love. This is why **love is more appropriately defined as a decision and not only a feeling.** Feelings come and go, but when you hit disillusionment and the feelings of love fade, sacramental marriage calls you to make a choice to love. When you make sacrifices and go out of your way to love the other person when you don't "feel" like loving, that is when you begin to change your situation of disillusionment and move towards joy.

Joy is a rewarding part of the cycle for couples who have consciously worked through their difficulties for the sake of their relationship. It is learning to trust and believe in the other person and beginning to know deep in your heart that you are loved - no matter what. It is the result of sacrificing, forgiving and communicating through the problems for the good of the marriage.

keeping romance alive

Think of your first year together as "getting off to a good start." Avoid extra commitments which require the two of you to spend lots of time apart; instead choose to spend more time together. Continue getting to know each other's thoughts and feelings, and exploring each other's communication styles. Have fun together and keep the romance alive. Some couples set up weekly dates in order to prioritize their time together. Learn to pray together and include God as an important partner in your marriage. Use this first year to build a firm foundation for your marriage.

 1. Describe one of the best dates you have had with your fiancé.

 2. What is the most romantic thing your fiancé has done for you? What is the most romantic thing you have done for your fiancé?

 3. What is different about your fiancé that lets you know that they are just right for you?

 4. List five things you can do in the course of an ordinary week to keep the romance alive when you're married.

love is a decision

If love were as fleeting as a feeling, people would "fall" into and out of love all the time. Relationships would never last. Love is an action word, not only a feeling word. When we are enjoying romance and feeling close to our spouse it is very easy to make decisions to love by putting the other first and our needs and wants second. When we live love as a decision we take responsibility for the relationship. We make the choice to put our spouse and our relationship before any issues. **We decide that the marriage is more important than being right, doing things our way, or "winning this one."** Making decisions to love means we make sacrifices for the sake of the other; forgiving rather than holding a grudge; listening rather than being distracted; instead of "giving in" we make the decision to "give" without resentment or expecting anything in return. Love becomes our unconditional gift.

NOW YOU'RE A COUPLE...

On your wedding day the two of you will begin a new life together. Creating and shaping this new life as a married couple is exciting and enriching. You come together as single people with your own lives, friends and interests; however, part of the vows you take include "forsaking all others."

Some people choose to live their lives as "married singles." This choice indicates an attitude that individual needs come before the marriage. This may be expressed through separate social, recreational and financial lives; that is, a general sense of separateness in living your lives. Marriage requires changes to these separate lifestyles in order to create your own married lifestyle. This will necessitate a change in priorities. Your spouse comes first.

Once you are married, spend more time with your spouse rather than with other friends. Working excessive overtime at your job should give way to more time spent with your spouse. Instead of participating in separate ball teams, you may choose to join a couples' team. However you shape your married life, it will require making sacrifices and compromises that will surely be rewarding and life-giving for your marriage.

 What is one change you anticipate making after you are married in order to have quality time with your spouse? (e.g. activities, friends, job, school, volunteer commitments, etc.)

 What is one area of your individual life that you would like to keep the same?

overcoming disillusionment

 7. The video makes it clear that in all marriages problems will occur. Mary Hengen indicated that people who are rigid do not do well handling problems. Rigid people believe they are always right. They do not want to "give in." They insist on having their way. They must have the last word.

• Are there any areas in which you would describe yourself as rigid? If so, what are they?

• Are there any areas in which you would describe your fiancé as rigid? If so, what are they?

OBSTACLES TO ACHIEVING JOY

• being rigid

• living as married singles

• living love as a feeling rather than as a decision

• having other 'gods'

• letting romance slide

• giving up

• leaving God out

• inability to handle anger or conflict

• ignoring addictions/ compulsions

---

 8. Think of how you have handled disillusionment in another area of your life. (job, college, personal/family)

 Check all that apply.

_____ complain	_____ wallowed in self pity
_____ advice from a counselor	_____ forgave
_____ criticize	_____ learned a lesson
_____ discuss with parents	_____ ended the relationship poorly
_____ got drunk/used drugs/over ate	_____ talked with a friend
_____ prayed	_____ exercised

9. Looking at what you've done in the past, how do you hope to handle future disillusionment?

10. God can help you overcome self-centeredness for the good of your marriage. What role do you want God to have in the day-to-day circumstances of your marriage?

- [ ] a full partnership with my spouse and myself
- [ ] only when we get into trouble
- [ ] I will leave it up to my spouse
- [ ] none

11. List ideas for making the decision to love your fiancé when:

you feel hurt by your fiancé:

your fiancé feels hurt by something you said or did:

you want to be alone and your fiancé wants to go out together:

you are angry with your fiancé:

your fiancé is angry with you:

12. The video brought home the point that everyone has a "god" that may become an obstacle to intimacy in marriage. Anytime that you put some "thing" ahead of your spouse you have a false god. Some examples include: TV (couch potato), sports, shopping and internet chat rooms. What is there in your life that may be a hindrance to a successful marriage?

- Is there something you recognize in your spouse's life that may be a deterrent to a strong marriage?

- What steps can you take to prevent problems from arising in these areas?

Married couples uniquely make God real to their spouses in how they live their Sacrament. Through mutual self-giving, respect, faithfulness and commitment, married couples love with the heart and mind of Jesus Christ and are loved in return. This Christ-like love opens their eyes and hearts to a deeper understanding and experience of God's love. Mary Hengen shared her lack of faith and belief in God when she and Phil were engaged and in the early years of marriage. By understanding her need and ability to trust in Phil, Mary experienced the love and faithfulness of God.

In Chapter One, you heard that in marriage your spouse "puts flesh on God." Literally this means you can experience the love of God through your future spouse. When you first realized that you wanted to be with this person for the rest of your life, what did you experience? Many people have reported that the other person made them more energized, more free to be who they are, and brought out their best qualities. Did you realize that is how God is already acting in your relationship? As you grow together in marriage you will come to see the presence of God more and more in each other.

What are some specific ways you've already experienced the unconditional love of God through your fiancé?

The following pages explore various addictions and compulsions people may have. Not only do these addictions make it difficult to achieve a successful marriage, they may **cause** disillusionment, or develop in an attempt to **escape** disillusionment. This section includes a wide range of topics such as alcohol abuse, sexual addiction, physical/emotional abuse, compulsive gambling, eating disorders, chemical/drug dependency and compulsive shopping. Since **denial** is one of the key elements of most addictions or abuse, **all couples should complete the pages that follow on addictions**.

Many couples ask "Is it normal to have doubts about entering a lifelong marriage?" It is normal if you are wondering about the awesomeness of the commitment. It is not normal if you are wondering about your fiance's questionable behavior.

Phil and Mary Hengen, Marriage and Family Therapists in private practice, make the point in the video, that in marriages where one or both spouses have an addiction, it is difficult to make the marriage work. They state however, that people in **recovery** clearly **can** have wonderful marriages.

In today's American culture, there are many things people become addicted to that do not seem to be an issue before marriage: It seems "normal" to many people to...

* Go out every weekend and drink to excess (Weekends start on Wednesday, right?)

* "Relax" by smoking pot or using crack/cocaine

* Spend excessive hours surfing the net

* Use chat rooms and email to feel alive and connected

* Search for online pornography and sex

* Shop 'til you drop (Plastic's not "real" money!)

* Always need the newest "toy"

* Hit the casinos several times a week

* Overeat (the national pastime)

* Huddle with other smokers outside, even if it is 0 degree weather

As you prepare for Sacramental marriage, take stock of your emotional and physical health in a new way. Explore habits you have that may become problems and adversely affect your relationship. Deal with them NOW in order to have the happiest marriage imaginable.

The following pages contain information about addictions and compulsions. Please read them over and if you find any of these patterns present in your life, you are urged to get help before you enter marriage. **Remember, if there is a problem before marriage, it will NOT get better just because you get married.** If you find that you are concerned about yourself or your fiancé, please communicate about the problem and begin the recovery process. National resources are listed. Please consult your local phone directory, the internet and other resources for ways to begin taking positive steps towards recovery.

Why would anyone knowingly marry someone with an addiction or compulsion? You might be surprised to know that those who come from clearly dysfunctional families almost seem unable to stop themselves from being attracted to those who most need to be taken care of. These are patterns they are accustomed to seeing in their lives and/or homes. This can be a real cause of trouble, but it is not always obvious to the individual. The life-long co-dependent, despite a desire to have a healthy  relationship, will be attracted to a person who fulfills their need to care-take others. This can be a disaster waiting to happen. Rarely are these marriages successful. Rather, it is inevitable that the individual with the problem will gradually advance into their addiction, while their co-dependent partner enables (buys beer for the alcoholic) or attempts to control the spouse.

DENIAL

A key symptom of abuse or addiction is denial. Sometimes, denial is present in both individuals. We've all heard the phrase, "Love is blind," and that is especially true in the case of the person in love with someone who suffers from an addiction or compulsion. Despite the presence of symptoms, they will ignore or look beyond that which is staring them right in the face. They will make excuses, seeing their future partner as a victim or as someone who's just had some bad breaks; whatever allows them to shut out information that might otherwise be a red flag. **Sometimes "love" allows one to shut out the voices of parents, friends and common sense.** Addressing addiction and compulsion issues needs to happen before marriage, not after! It is also important that there be ongoing evaluation – it does NOT just "go away." Here is a simple way to look at the situation:

What are the two primary ingredients of a successful marriage?

Give up?

Two healthy people!

If you suspect that you or your fiancé has a problem please do not ignore it or allow yourself to be manipulated into minimizing or denying it. The following self-tests can be used to help someone break through their denial and recognize whether or not they need to take action.

are you chemically dependent?

"Substance abuse has become one of the most common problems in American families today. It is a major cause of family disruption and divorce. Before individuals marry, issues with chemical dependency need to be resolved. In order for that to be the case, it is important to know how to recognize abuse or addiction.

Ask yourself the following questions and answer them as honestly as you can.

	Yes	No
• Have you ever skipped school, class or work to get high?	☐	☐
• I try to keep others from knowing how much I drink/use.	☐	☐
• I get drunk/stoned when I didn't intend to.	☐	☐
• Are your friends hassling you about getting high?	☐	☐
• Have you ever felt bad after using drugs/alcohol?	☐	☐
• Does using cause you money problems?	☐	☐
• Do you pick your friends by their use of drugs/alcohol?	☐	☐
• Does your use of drugs make you careless of your family's welfare?	☐	☐
• Have you stopped doing things because you use drugs or alcohol?	☐	☐
• Do you crave (want) to get high at a certain time daily?	☐	☐
• I drink/use drugs first thing when I get up after sleep?	☐	☐
• Does using cause you to have difficulty sleeping or staying awake?	☐	☐
• Once I start drinking/drugging, it's difficult to stop.	☐	☐
• Has using caused you to drop out of school or is it risking your job?	☐	☐
• I am able to drink/drug more than I used to?	☐	☐
• Do you get high alone?	☐	☐
• Have you ever had a loss of memory as a result of using?	☐	☐
• Has a doctor ever treated you for anything because of using?	☐	☐
• I eat little or irregularly while drinking/drugging.	☐	☐
• Have you ever been to a hospital or institution because of using drugs or drinking?	☐	☐

Any yes answers are cause for concern. yes to 3 or more questions is a strong indication of the need for professional help."[1] Contacting organizations listed in the back of this book will give you further information.

do you have a gambling problem?

"Not everyone who gambles develops a problem. There is a certain percentage of gamblers for whom the activity causes problems in different areas of life and for some, becomes uncontrollable. Compulsive gambling has been shown to be a chronic, progressive and terribly disabling disorder that creates an overwhelming, irresistible impulse to gamble. It is diagnosable and treatable.

Signs and symptoms of the disorder range from occasional to frequent or even constant behaviors which may include:

* **A periodic or constant loss of control over gambling.**

* **Progressive increase in the amount wagered or put at risk.**

* **Preoccupation with gambling or obtaining the money to gamble.**

* **Gambling to escape feeling badly.**

* **Irrational thinking, lying, and committing illegal acts, for gambling funds.**

* **Continuing the behavior despite adverse consequences.**

Gambler's Anonymous has 20 questions it asks of new members. Compulsive gamblers usually answer "yes" to at least seven of the questions.

	Yes	No
• Did you lose time from work due to gambling?	☐	☐
• Has gambling ever made your home life unhappy?	☐	☐
• Did gambling affect your reputation?	☐	☐
• Have you ever felt remorse after gambling?	☐	☐
• Did you ever gamble to get money with which to pay debts or otherwise solve financial difficulties?	☐	☐
• After losing, did you feel you must return as soon as possible to win back your losses?	☐	☐
• After a win, did you have a strong urge to return to win more?	☐	☐
• Did you often gamble until your last dollar was gone?	☐	☐
• Have you ever sold anything to finance your gambling?	☐	☐
• Were you reluctant to use "gambling money" for normal expenditures?	☐	☐
• Did gambling make you careless of the welfare of yourself or your family?	☐	☐
• Did you ever gamble longer than you had planned?	☐	☐
• Have you ever gambled to escape worry or trouble?	☐	☐
• Have you ever committed or considered committing an illegal act to finance gambling?	☐	☐
• Did gambling cause you to have difficulty sleeping?	☐	☐
• Do arguments, disappointment, or frustrations create within you the urge to gamble?	☐	☐
• Do you ever have an urge to celebrate any good fortune by a few hours of gambling?	☐	☐
• Have you ever considered self-destruction as a result of your gambling?	☐	☐

A "problem gambler" usually answers 4 to 6 questions with a yes.
A pathological (compulsive) gambler usually answers yes to seven or more.
If you've assessed yourself or your fiancé and find that you have answered yes to more than 4, you've got a problem. Seek help and clarification. Attend open meetings of Gamblers Anonymous.

The impact of problem gambling on family and individuals is staggering. Family problems abound: poor communication, strained finances, dishonesty and manipulation, stress-related illness, neglect, divorce and abandonment often result. "(2) Do not let this problem impact your marriage. If you feel you or your fiancé have a problem, seek help BEFORE being married."

do you have an eating disorder?

"Disordered eating is when a person's attitudes about food, weight and body size lead to very rigid eating and exercise habits that jeopardize one's health, happiness and safety. Disordered eating may begin as a way to lose a few pounds or get in shape, but these behaviors can quickly get out of control, become obsessions or even turn into an eating disorder.

	Yes	No
• Do you avoid eating meals or snacks when you're around other people?	☐	☐
• Do you constantly calculate numbers of fat grams and calories?	☐	☐
• Do you weigh yourself often and find yourself obsessed with the number on the scale?	☐	☐
• Do you exercise because you feel like you have to, not because you want to?	☐	☐
• Are you afraid of gaining weight?	☐	☐
• Do you ever feel out of control when you are eating?	☐	☐
• Do your eating patterns include extreme dieting, preferences for certain foods, withdrawn or ritualized behavior at mealtime, or secretive binging?	☐	☐
• Has weight loss, dieting, and/or control of food become one of your major concerns?	☐	☐
• Do you feel ashamed, disgusted, or guilty after eating?	☐	☐
• Do you worry about the weight, shape or size of your body?	☐	☐
• Do you feel like your identity and value is based on how you look or how much you weigh?	☐	☐

If you answered yes to any of these questions, you could be dealing with disordered eating. It is likely that these attitudes and behaviors are taking a toll on your mental and physical well being. It is important that you start to talk about your eating habits and concerns now, rather than waiting until your situation gets more serious than you can handle."(3) Check the resources for additional information.

is violence or abuse part of your relationship?

"Domestic violence is behavior – emotional, psychological, physical or sexual abuse – that one person in an intimate relationship uses in order to control the other. It takes many different forms and includes behavior such as threats, name-calling, isolation, withholding of money, actual or threatened physical harm and sexual assault. Most domestic violence is committed against women by their male partners," but it can be the other way around.

There are many reasons why an individual may abuse (try to control) his/her partner. Often the person was raised in a home where they saw and experienced abuse. New ways of relating will have to be learned if this was the case and a marriage should be postponed until recovery is well underway and a support system in place. Remember, a person in "recovery" can make a loving and beautiful marriage. The following checklist may help you decide if your relationship has some of the symptoms of domestic abuse.

"Does your fiancé:

	Yes	No
• Constantly criticize you and your abilities as a partner, parent or employee? [Name-calling or put-downs]	☐	☐
• Behave in an over-protective manner or become extremely jealous?	☐	☐
• Threaten to hurt you, your children, pets, family members, friends or herself/himself?	☐	☐
• Prevent you from seeing family or friends? [isolation]	☐	☐
• Get suddenly angry or "lose her/his temper?"	☐	☐
• Destroy personal property or throw things around?	☐	☐
• Deny you access to family assets like bank accounts, credit cards, the car or control all finances and force you to account for what you spend? [withholding money]	☐	☐
• Use intimidation or manipulation to control you or your children? Hit, punch, slap, kick, shove, choke or bite you?	☐	☐
• Prevent you from going where you want to go, when you want to and with whomever you want?	☐	☐
• Make you have sex when you don't want to or do things sexually that you do not want to do? [sexual assault]	☐	☐
• Humiliate or embarrass you in front of other people?	☐	☐

If you said **yes** to ANY of these questions, you may be a victim of domestic violence or abuse."(4) You must heed these common warning signs. The batterer uses acts of violence and a series of behaviors, including intimidation, threats, psychological abuse, isolation, etc. to coerce and control the other person. The violence may not happen often but it remains as a hidden and constant terrorizing factor. In a Sacramental marriage, a husband should be "loving his wife, as he does his own body" and a wife will be "one flesh" with her husband. This union will be marked with generosity, deferring to one another with gentle love.

do you have a sexual addiction?

"Though the idea of sexual addiction is new to many, sex is increasingly understood as another in the growing list of addictive means people use to reduce isolation, lack of emotion and tension; to resolve conflict, gain power and provide escape; or supply false emotional and spiritual security.

Early on, many of us came to feel disconnected – from parents, peers and ourselves. We tuned out with fantasy and masturbation. We plugged in by drinking in the pictures, the images and pursuing the objects of our fantasies. We lusted and wanted to be lusted after. We became true addicts: sex with self, promiscuity, adultery, dependency relationships and more fantasy. We got it through the eyes, we bought it, sold it, traded it and gave it away. We were addicted to the intrigue, the tease, the forbidden. The only way we knew to be free of it, was to do it. "Please connect with me and make me whole!" we cried with outstretched arms ...

Our habit made true intimacy impossible. We could never know real union with another because we were addicted to the unreal. We went for the "chemistry," the connection that had the magic, because it by-passed intimacy and true union. Fantasy corrupted the real; lust killed love.

Test yourself:

	Yes	No
• Have you ever thought you needed help for your sexual thinking or behavior?	☐	☐
• Have you ever thought that you'd be better off if you did not keep "giving in?"	☐	☐
• Have you ever thought that sex or stimuli are controlling you?	☐	☐
• Have you ever tried to stop or limit doing what you felt was wrong in your sexual behavior?	☐	☐
• Do you resort to sex to escape, relieve anxiety or because you can't cope?	☐	☐
• Do you feel guilt, remorse or depression afterward?	☐	☐
• Has your pursuit of sex become more compulsive?	☐	☐
• Does your pursuit of sex interfere with relations with your spouse?	☐	☐
• Do you have to resort to images or memories during sex?	☐	☐
• Does an irresistible impulse arise when the other party makes the overtures or sex is offered?	☐	☐
• Do you keep going from one 'relationship' to another?	☐	☐
• Do you feel the "right relationship" would help you stop lusting, masturbating or being so promiscuous?	☐	☐
• Do you have a destructive need-a desperate sexual or emotional need for someone?	☐	☐
• Does pursuit of sex make you careless for yourself or the welfare of your family or others?	☐	☐
• Has your effectiveness or concentration decreased as sex has become more compulsive?	☐	☐
• Do you lose time from work for it?	☐	☐
• Do you turn to a lower environment when pursuing sex?	☐	☐

	Yes	No
• Do you want to get away from the sex partner as soon as possible after the act?	☐	☐
• Although your spouse is sexually compatible, do you still masturbate or have sex with others?	☐	☐
• Have you ever been arrested for a sex-related offense?"(5)	☐	☐

If you have noticed that your fiance visits adult bookstores, looks at pornography, has an interest in pedophilia (sex with a child), or if you are aware that they have been involved in an incest relationship (sex with a family member), or visits massage parlors it is very important that you lovingly communicate your concerns and insist that before marriage the person get professional and spiritual help and begin recovery with Sexaholics Anonymous.

Today, we have a particularly virulent form of peeping tom/exhibitionism and sex available to everyone on the internet. If you are aware that your fiancé is using the internet inappropriately, has had anonymous sex (with a stranger) or uses the internet for sexual gratification it is very important that you postpone the wedding and seek help.

are you a shopaholic?

"Shop 'til you drop." This is not a person who is shopping the sales and buys carefully, but a person who chronically overspends in a compulsive manner. Do any of these qualities apply to you?

	Yes	No
• I use shopping as a form of entertainment.	☐	☐
• I feel anxious when I am not shopping.	☐	☐
• I go shopping when I am having a hard time dealing with life.	☐	☐
• Shopping replaces talking and feeling and makes unpleasant problems go away.	☐	☐
• Others have questioned my shopping and spending habits.	☐	☐
• I often buy things I don't need or want.	☐	☐
• I get a rush from shopping and I think about it all the time.	☐	☐
• I hide things I buy from my family.	☐	☐
• I make sure no one sees the bills from my shopping.	☐	☐
• I often do not tell my family what I have brought home.	☐	☐
• Shopping is a major part of my life.	☐	☐

"Using" shopping as an answer to stress, unhappiness, emptiness or as your major form of entertainment can end up causing you many problems, only one of which is financial.(6)

In closing, you will find pages for secular help in the back of the book. Additionally, there are many ways that the Church can help when you find yourself with a problem. Jesus Christ is the great healer and helper of all. Seek Jesus in prayer and call upon the people of the Church for support. Having a spiritual director, a person who will pray with you and listen to you on a regular basis can be a wonderful source of support. Your pastor or priest, the professional agencies of the Church and many Catholic counselors are available to offer you support so that your recovery and marriage will be built on the solid ground of the love of God and God's people.

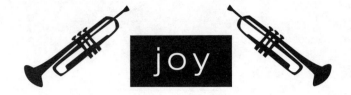

joy

Joy requires having been through disillusionment and coming out on the other side.

a decision to ... run

Perhaps you are a runner. When you first began running you were exhilarated, the wind in your hair, your heart pounding; pushing yourself day-by-day to achieve a strength with running that you never imagined you would have. You looked forward to your running time; you were crazy about running! Then it became real work. Perhaps because you expected too much of yourself.

Perhaps your coach expected even more. Goals taunted you. You got bogged down. Practicing every day in the hot sun, feeling your body being punished in ways you would not have imagined, every muscle aching. Is it worth it??? Do you really want to do this? Then perhaps you began to re-think it. Your motivation shifted. You received more training from the coach. And as you continued, as you practiced, as you learned, running became effortless. Your body strengthened, your lungs expanded, your mind adjusted. You began to notice the wind in your hair, you were exhilarated again. This was a different exhilaration ... borne of patience, grace and maturity.

"Joy is the understanding and trust that years of togetherness has produced. An intimacy shared by simply being together. Joy is love !"

Bob Edwards

"When I am with my husband I feel content and peaceful. It is being together and not even needing to talk, just feeling close and enjoying a shared history of almost 40 years of knowing each other."

Susan Edwards

Engaged couples have not experienced the kind of joy we are talking about. You have surely experienced romance, the excitement of falling in love. You may have begun to have times of disillusionment ... when you wondered if you wanted to continue in the relationship. You are just beginning "training" and will continue "practicing." The stage of joy is something that is the result of a life shared together. It takes more time than any of you have had, yet. It is a grace and a reward. A time in the relationship born of working together through the good times and the bad, the struggles and the successes, the worries and wonders. It is something you achieve together. It reflects a peace that comes from deep inside you, from a place of patience, grace and maturity.

 We are not asking questions about your own joy because you probably have yet to experience it. Can you think of a married couple in your life that is living in the stage of joy?

Michelangelo once said...

"I saw the angel in the marble and carved until I set him free."(7) The stages of a relationship can be compared to a piece of marble. During the romance of the beginning, a sculptor has a beautiful piece of marble ... lovely to look at and a treasure to own. As time goes on disillusionment sets in as the sculptor begins to chip away at the stone noticing the cracks and imperfections; it is hard to imagine the finished creation. Through the years the sculptor continues to work the marble and a beautiful piece of art is discovered just like the joy of the relationship. The beauty that was hidden is revealed.

At the end of the day, if we feel things have not gone well, we can agree to start over and do it differently tomorrow.

SEX AND
Chapter 4: SEXUALITY

HAVE YOU COME
TOGETHER FREELY

What makes a married couple's relationship different than that of two close friends?

Sexual intimacy as an expression of their love, openness to children and their **commitment to one another for life** are unique aspects of a married relationship.

" [Conjugal love] aims at a deeply personal unity, a unity that, beyond union in one flesh, leads to forming one heart and soul; it demands *indissolubility* and *faithfulness* in definitive mutual giving; and it is open to *fertility*. "

Familiaris Consortio 13 (1)

The intimacy of married sexuality is a unique way of expressing love, commitment, fidelity and trust. The act of intercourse is intended to more deeply unite the couple through their expression of love and to be life-giving to their marriage. "...Two become one flesh" is most literally fulfilled in the act of marital intercourse with the creation of new life, children. Sexual love is an example of God's creative power at work in our lives. It is a precious and beautiful gift. Sex is good, sacred and holy. It renews and deepens the existing bond between husband and wife.

This powerful gift of sexual love has the potential to fulfill physical and emotional needs; to serve as a strong communication tool; to facilitate forgiveness and healing; to bring joy, peace and harmony. However, the flip side of this gift is the potential to hurt through misunderstandings, abuse and self-centeredness. The marital sexual relationship has been described as a barometer that clearly reflects the state of the entire relationship.

As an engaged couple, **are you like the Odom's, who did not believe sex would be an issue in their marriage?** The 2000 Survey, *Time, Sex and Money: The First Five Years of Marriage* revealed the second greatest problematic issue in the first five years of marriage was "frequency of sexual relations," second only to communication. (2)

"...Two shall become One flesh"

Matthew 19:5

The questions in this section can help you begin communicating about your expectations, feelings, fears, concerns, hopes and needs.

attitudes

Check those statements that describe your attitudes. Then go back and
star those statements that you believe describe your fiancé's attitude.

1.

- ◯ Sex should be spontaneous and not planned.

- ◯ The husband should be the primary initiator for sex.

- ◯ Neither partner should ever say "no."

- ◯ The woman should determine frequency of intercourse.

- ◯ It is important to feel close before having sex.

- ◯ The husband is responsible for the woman's pleasure.

- ◯ Sex can be used as a reward.

- ◯ Sex can be used to resolve problems.

- ◯ After marriage, physical affection should always result in sexual intercourse.

- ◯ Abstaining periodically will keep our sex life passionate.

- ◯ Sex is considered a failure if both partners do not climax.

- ◯ Sex is more important to the husband.

- ◯ After being married awhile, sex will happen less frequently.

- ◯ The quality of sex is more important than frequency.

- ◯ Sex should not be talked about.

- ◯ Sexual intercourse is only for having babies.

- ◯ A satisfying sexual relationship is essential for a happy marriage.

- ◯ Sex will be boring after awhile.

- ◯ Sex will always be beautiful and special.

During your discussion of this section be sure to review each

statement and discuss any differences based on your answers.

family of origin issues

Diverse upbringings influence your attitudes about sexuality, including how you show affection, the expectations and roles of the husband and wife, as well as openness in talking about sexual issues. In some families, sex was never discussed; in others it was talked about openly, while still others were raised to think sex was "dirty" or a chore.

 Describe how your Family of Origin treated sexuality (e.g. forbidden subject, no show of affection, fun activity, a beautiful expression of love, a joke, dirty, chore, etc.).

 How has this influenced your attitudes regarding sex?

everyday sexuality

Contrary to how society depicts sexuality, a married couple's sexual relationship is not limited to the bedroom. Sexuality involves who we are as male and female, with diverse needs, expectations, perspectives, ways of communicating and showing affection. You need to understand the influence that American culture has on your life through the media, music, TV, etc. There, sex is often portrayed as merely an activity that provides entertainment or physical satisfaction to couples. But your sexuality involves much more than intercourse. **Sexuality involves total giving to one another in love, from the moment you wake up to the moment you fall asleep. It is how you respect, love, touch and treat each other all day, every day.** Your sexuality is indeed a special, unique gift from God. Couples who use sex merely for physical gratification (whether dating or married) will have a difficult time recognizing their sexuality as the most intimate and life-giving expression of love that can occur in a married relationship.

" ...My lover belongs to *me* and *I* to *him*..."

Song of Songs 2:16

building relational intimacy

Emotional - relating together on the feeling level including hopes and dreams

Social - enjoying being together as friends, sharing activities, interests

Intellectual - listening to one another and discussing important issues

Sexual - deeply physical self-giving, with mutual trust, love, and devotion

Spiritual - deeply personal sharing of faith and beliefs; shared prayer (3)

The video brought out that "making love" begins from the moment you wake up and involves gentleness, kindness, affection and loving interaction without the expectation that it must lead to intercourse. A married couple needs to be attentive to one another and in touch with each other's needs. It is being together and being connected in all ways as you go about your lives, doing all the regular things that people do.

 4. Name 1 or 2 "little favors" that you can do each day to show affection for your partner.

 5. What kind of affection is important to you?

 6. What kind of affection do you believe is important to your fiancé?

 7. Describe your sexual needs and desires other than intercourse.

 8. What do you find most physically attractive about your fiancé?

 9. What do you think he/she finds most physically attractive about you?

Holy Scripture affirms that man and woman were created for one another: *"It is not good that the man should be alone."* (Gen 2:18) The woman, *"flesh of his flesh,"* i.e., his equal, his nearest in all things, is given to him by God as a "helpmate"; she thus represents God from whom comes our help. (Cf. Gen 2:18-25)

Catechism of the Catholic Church 1605

YOUR **SEXUALITY** IS **GOOD. SEX** IS A **HOLY** EXPRESSION OF YOUR **LOVE** FOR ONE ANOTHER. God created us male and female. Christ instituted the Sacrament of Matrimony and calls spouses to total, mutual self-giving in all aspects of their relationship, including sex. In the video, Fr. Vomund talked about the marital sexual relationship being characterized by integrity. **Integrity** means there is strength of character, honesty, honor, goodness, respect and responsibility. It also means that there is no abuse, infidelity, manipulation, disrespect or using the other solely for physical gratification.

 Do you believe you can characterize your future married relationship as possessing **integrity**? Do you anticipate any problems?

"And have joy of the wife of your youth,
  your lovely hind, your graceful doe.
Her love will invigorate you always,
  through her love you will flourish continually.
When you lie down she will watch over you,
  and when you wake she will share your concerns;
  wherever you turn, she will guide you.**"**

Proverbs 5:18-19, 6:22

expectations

11. How often do you think you will have sexual relations in a day? a week? a month?

12. How would you describe a satisfying sexual relationship?

13. What types of sexual acts would make you uncomfortable?

14. Name 1 or 2 circumstances under which you might say "no" to sexual relations.

15. How might you feel if your spouse says "no"?

16. Based on your answers above, do you believe your expectations are realistic?

A balanced lifestyle includes staying in the best shape physically, spiritually and emotionally. As you begin your new life together it is beneficial for both of you to be in the best of health. Maintaining your good health now will increase your chances of a long life together. A physical examination for each of you is in order before your wedding, including pap smear and gynecologic examination for women. Additionally, recording the woman's fertility changes is a good way to monitor her health and to provide early detection of gynecologic problems (for more information see page 101).

Now is the time to take proactive steps toward good sexual health. Any conditions that are identified can be investigated before your marriage because they may signal health problems or possible difficulty related to having children.

DEVELOP GOOD HEALTH CARE HABITS

The American Cancer Society recommends monthly self-examination of the breasts, annual pap smears and monthly testicular self-examinations. Following these practices can help you maintain optimum health and result in better treatment options and outcomes, should a problem arise. It is important to remember that your sexual health is a part of your overall health. For a long lifetime together, don't neglect either one.

SEXUALLY TRANSMITTED DISEASES

Did you know that if you or your fiancé has ever had any genital contact with anyone else, you are already at risk for having contracted a sexually transmitted disease (STD)? This "contact" doesn't have to have been full intercourse; STD's can be transmitted by genital skin-to skin contact, through some bodily fluids and by oral-genital contact as well. If you have been genitally active in the past, you bring the exposure with that individual and all the individuals he or she has ever been with, to your marriage. You owe it to yourself to be tested and treated, if needed.

Here are some sobering facts from the Centers for Disease Control:

• One in every five Americans are presently infected with an STD.

• Sixty-three percent of all STDs occur in persons under 25 years of age.

• An infected person may go for weeks, months, even years without symptoms.

• Some STDs can be passed to children during the birthing process.

• Many STDs (such as chlamydia) can cause infertility in both men and women.

• Eighty percent of those who are infected do not know they have a disease (and can pass it on!)(4)

Now for some encouraging news:

• Some STDs are easily treated with a simple course of antibiotics; the sooner, the better.

• Early detection increases your chance of saving your health and fertility.

• You **can** be pro-active and get a complete screening **now** and, if necessary, get treatment.

• You have the right, responsibility and ability to protect yourself and the ones you love.

• Knowledge is power, so get informed and stay healthy.

Protecting your sexual health and your fertility should be a priority in your marriage. Don't assume that just because you've been to see a doctor that you have been tested. Routine physicals (pap smears, etc.) do not test for all sexually transmitted diseases. You must specifically request to be tested for STDs. Testing is available through local healthcare providers. If you learn you are infected with an STD, seek treatment immediately. You may also want to seek support from friends, family, supportive clergy or a counseling professional. Protect yourself, your fiancé and your future children by getting tested and treated. You'll be glad you did!

17.

How do you think any past sexual relationships will affect your marriage? For yourself? For your spouse?

18.

If there are past sexual relationships, have the two of you discussed any potential risk for HIV/AIDS or other sexually transmitted diseases? Have you been tested to protect your future spouse? If not, why not?

 Do you presently participate in, or have you participated in, any activities that may contribute to problems in your sexual relationship?

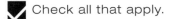 Check all that apply.

___ pornography

___ homosexual fantasies/activities

___ strip clubs

___ prostitution

___ masturbation

___ voyeurism (watching others participating in sexual acts— live, movies, TV, computer)

___ casual sex/ one-night stands

___ abortion

___ phone/internet sex

___ victim or perpetrator of sexual abuse

___ sexual addiction

___ exhibitionism (wet t-shirt contest, putting yourself on display)

Any type of sexual addiction will make it difficult, if not impossible for a married couple to have a healthy sexual relationship. Be sure to complete the questionnaire in the section on addictions, in Chapter 3 on page 38.

 If you checked any of the above, have you talked with your fiancé about it?

If you currently participate in any of the above, are you willing to seek counseling? If not, why not?

planning your bachelor/bachelorette party

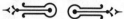

A gathering of close friends for a bachelor/bachelorette party is a tradition in our culture. The type of party you plan should reflect the quality of your relationship with your future spouse and the mature commitment you are making. Society sometimes looks at this very differently. As you think about bonding or re-bonding with close friends during your last weeks as a "single adult" consider how you can share some healthy good times that will be good memories for the rest of your life. Here are some suggestions!

A day or evening...

HIS	HERS	AVOID
Restaurant/arcade (i.e. Dave and Busters)	Day Spa	Drinking in excess
Golf	Luncheon	Strippers
Go-carting	Lingerie Party	Casual sex
Card games/Game night	Game night	Pornography
Basketball	Movie night	Compromising situations
Football	Dinner/dancing	Voyeurism/exhibitionism
Sporting events	Sporting events	Illegal activities

 Describe your ideal bachelor/bachelorette party. Some time in the next week discuss this with your fiancé.

Be sure to make your wishes known to others involved in celebrating with you!

> "*The unity of marriage,* distinctly recognized by our Lord, is made clear in the equal personal dignity which must be accorded to **man and wife** in mutual and unreserved affection."
>
> *Gaudium et Spes* 49.2 (5)

it's all about control...

✖ **Sarah never imagined marriage would be like this.**
Now she can look back at their dating time and see the warning signs. John always wanted to know where she was and who she talked to. He took up all her time and she slowly drifted away from her friends. Then she thought his jealous nature was romantic. She now knows it is sick. She feels isolated and alone, almost like a prisoner. When they dated, John lost his temper often, it seemed usually for no reason. He always apologized and brought flowers or a little gift the next day. Now John's temper tantrums occur daily and there's never an apology. She can never predict what might set him off - dirty dishes, his favorite TV program being a rerun; the most inconsequential thing. It's like walking on egg shells. And she is always the target of his anger. The vulgar names he calls her just get worse and worse and now she is filled with self-doubt and is beginning to believe she is as worthless as John says she is. Sarah feels hopeless and helpless to get out of this nightmare. Her family would never believe what was happening to her.

FACT:

About 6 million women are victims of domestic abuse each year.

(6)

FACT:

Domestic violence occurs among all races and all socioeconomic groups.

(7)

FACT:

Abuse comes in many disguises... sexual abuse and rape (even by spouses), physical, verbal, emotional abuse.

(7)

 23. Have you ever had a friend who you suspected may be in an abusive relationship? What did you see that made you suspect that this might be true? Did you take any action? If so, what?

 24. Have you noticed symptoms of abuse in your future spouse's family of origin? (Have you ever said, "Hey, you better not treat me the way your Dad treats your Mom – or your Mom treats your Dad."?)

25. Are you aware of any abusive situations in your own family or extended family?

 26. Does your fiancé treat you with respect and dignity? Give examples.

 27. Do you believe you may be at risk to become a victim of abuse in your marriage, be it verbal, physical, emotional or sexual?

If your gut tells you that you need to look into this further, DO IT!!!

Remember, you cannot expect that another person will change, or that you can change them after you are married. It is important to receive help and counseling BEFORE marriage, not just after.

Please consult a professional such as your doctor, mental health professional, a trusted priest, family member or friend who can assist you in receiving help. Refer to the Resource page for more information.

The parties to a marriage covenant are a baptized man and woman, free to contract marriage, who freely express their consent; "to be free" means:

✳ not being under constraint;
✳ not impeded by an natural or ecclesiastical law.

Catechism of the Catholic Church 1625

know anyone who is living together?

Cohabitation (living together outside of marriage) is very common in our society. Some feel that living together before marriage will help couples get to know each other better before deciding to marry. Living together, in their minds, often serves as a test for the relationship. Others live together for convenience, or with the intent to take their relationship to the "next level." Many like the open-ended lifestyle, the lack of commitment. In cohabitation many couples think they have the benefits of marriage without the problems. Often couples tell themselves that their marriage will be stronger because they have already lived together.

In the video, Fr. Jeff Vomund mentioned that if the Church were to write a script for your lives, it would not include cohabitation. The Catholic Church has always taught that cohabitation poses many problems for couples, adds risks to the marriage covenant and is contrary to the teachings of Christ. Part of the Church's concern is that: 1.) the sexual relationship has a different meaning outside of marriage; 2.) There appears to be no commitment, no intent to be open to children; 3.) God is basically left out of the equation. The research of many leading sociologists is now providing evidence validating the church's concerns. Some of their points include:

▶ **"Married couples who live together first are 50% more likely to divorce within a decade than those who don't."**(8)

▶ **No sacred bond exists. "In a study reported in the *Journal of Marriage and the Family*, the longer couples had lived together before marriage, the more unhappy they were after marriage."**(9)

▶ **With no marriage commitment, there is more to lose when there are major disagreements. Couples living together may tend to ignore major areas of disagreement to avoid confrontations that may lead to breakups.**(10)

▶ **Couples who live together usually are "less religious than couples who do not cohabit."**(10)

▶ **"The rate of domestic abuse in cohabitating relationships is far higher than in those who do not cohabitate."**(11)

▶ **Those who cohabitated prior to marriage "ranked constant bickering as a top problematic issue [in the first five years of marriage.] An issue not listed by those who had not cohabitated."**(12)

You have chosen to come to the Catholic Church for marriage preparation and to have a minister of the Church, as well as the community witness and support your marriage. The Church wants your marriage to be strong, faithful and blessed.

28. Which of the statements about cohabitation cause you concern?

 29. What were your reasons for choosing your current living situation?

"Have you come together freely and without reservation to give yourselves to each other in marriage?"
**Statement of Intention:
The Rite of Marriage**

 30. Why are you choosing to get married at this time?

- desire for commitment?
- ultimatum from one partner? ("marry me now or I am leaving you")
- desire to have children?
- family pressure?
- change in personal beliefs about the acceptability of cohabitation?
- financial reasons?
- other_____

 31. What do you expect will change after your wedding day?

 32. Are there any issues you have been avoiding for fear of "rocking the boat?" What are they?

 33. How would you characterize your faith/religious position?

 34. Can you invite God to be a greater partner in your marriage?

 35. If you are not completely free to say "no" to something, you are not really free to say "yes" to it. Do you have the genuine freedom to say a full "yes!" to this marriage if you are already sharing the bills, a couch, TV, a dog and the bedroom?

 36. Have you decided to abstain from sexual relations until your wedding day?

> The consent must be an act of the will of each of the contracting parties, free of coercion or grave external fear. (Cf. CIC, can. 1103.) No human power can substitute for this consent. (Cf. CIC, can. 1057. 1.) If this freedom is lacking the marriage is invalid.
>
> *Catechism of the Catholic Church* 1628

A CHALLENGE

The Catholic Church believes that the gift of sexual love belongs only in a married relationship, because it represents the total giving of self to another. The unique dignity and honor of this expression of love is intended by God to be fulfilled only in a married relationship, one that promises faithfulness, permanence and openness to life.

Fr. Vomund said the Church invites you to live with integrity and authenticity out of respect for your love and commitment. Therefore, in preparing to receive the Sacrament of Matrimony, the Church challenges you to move apart and/or to abstain from sexual relations until your wedding day.

Abstinence from sexual relations provides couples with opportunities to create and build romance outside the bedroom, to reinforce communication, and to renew and strengthen the relationship. Abstinence for non-married couples allows them to live their vocation as single people with the authenticity and integrity of which Fr. Vomund speaks.

Be just as good a **LOVER** out of the **bedroom** as in the **bedroom.**

Chapter 4:

Chapter 5:

COMMUNICATION

WITH GOD AND WITH EACH OTHER

FOR BETTER OR
FOR WORSE

Communication, marriage's #1 challenge, is the key to real intimacy.

The ability to share hopes, fears, needs, wants, expectations ... to convey love, affirmation, compassion ... to express hurts and disappointments ... to resolve disagreements ... is essential to a successful marriage. Good communication opens the door to trust, understanding and becoming one. The ability to communicate on many levels **is a skill that is learned**. People are not born with the natural ability to be skilled communicators. Learning communication skills takes practice, patience and resolve. It is giving the best of yourself to your spouse.

what's in your concrete?

Norman said...

"If we are going to start this marriage, we are going to start it right and we are going to use God as our foundation."

Some of the concrete for the foundation of your marriage is already churning in the mixer. The ingredients include your beliefs and ideas formed long ago, before you met one another. Use the following questions to explore the ingredients you already have.

 1. How important is faith in my life at this time?

◯ Very Important   ◯ Somewhat Important   ◯ Not very Important

2. Rate the following faith issues in your family of origin.

	Very Important	Somewhat Important	Not very Important
Belief in God			
Belief in Jesus Christ as God's Son			
Night prayers with parents			
Meal time prayers			
Attending church as a family			
Prayer as a family			
Individual prayer time			
Participating in church activities/programs			
Giving financial support to the church			
Inviting God's help in times of crisis or for making major decisions			
Reaching out to help others			

 3. Reflecting on the faith issues in your family of origin, what approaches to faith do you want to continue in your marriage? What approaches to faith do you want to change?

Obviously, there were things you saw that attracted you to your fiancé and made you desire a relationship with him/her. In the same way your image of God can attract you or cause you to turn away. Your view of God determines the role you will allow God to have in the foundation of your marriage.

 The image you have of God grows and changes throughout your life and affects all your relationships. What images of God are strongest for you right now.
Discuss one of these with your fiancé.

○ God is love.

○ God is the creator of all and giver of many gifts.

○ God is the just judge, punishing us for our sins.

○ God has a cold heart and allows the poor and innocent to suffer in the world.

○ God is always there, ready to help me.

○ God always lets me down when I'm in need.

○ God is a helpless bystander who watches us suffer.

○ God comforts me and supports me through life.

○ God has sent my fiancé to me.

○ Other_____

 Fr. Vomund stated in the video that praying together as a couple is THE most intimate thing a couple can do together, more than intercourse. Do you agree? Explain your answer.

 Sharing your hopes, dreams, needs and petitions in prayer with your fiancé can be uncomfortable and scary. Have you ever prayed with your fiancé? If not, are you willing to try? Select one of the suggestions from "So How Do We Do It?" on page 65 and try it this week!

 Fr. Vomund talked about the fact that couples who go to church together weekly and have an active prayer life together are far less likely to get divorced. Do you plan to go to Church together each week? Do you want to build a couple prayer life together?

Now that you have looked at what things are already in your mixer, you must decide together what ingredients you want to add to give your marriage the most solid foundation. Use the following questions to help you decide.

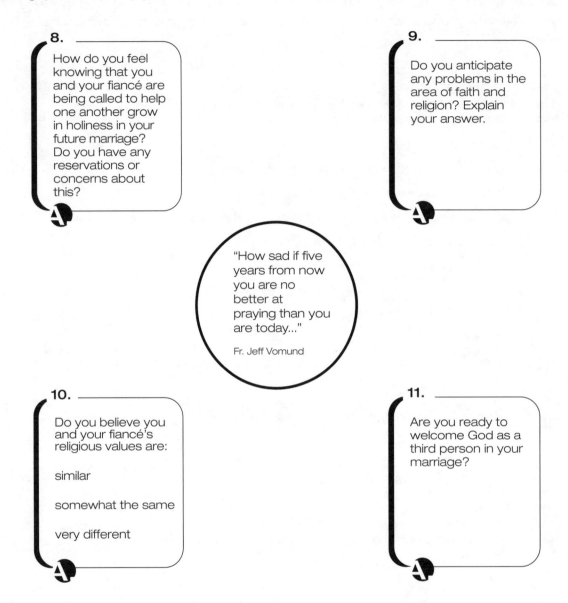

8. How do you feel knowing that you and your fiancé are being called to help one another grow in holiness in your future marriage? Do you have any reservations or concerns about this?

9. Do you anticipate any problems in the area of faith and religion? Explain your answer.

"How sad if five years from now you are no better at praying than you are today..."

Fr. Jeff Vomund

10. Do you believe you and your fiancé's religious values are:

similar

somewhat the same

very different

11. Are you ready to welcome God as a third person in your marriage?

By this grace[from the Sacrament of Matrimony] they [the married couple] "help one another to attain holiness in their married life and in welcoming and educating their children." (LG 11.2; cf. LG 41.)

Catechism of the Catholic Church #1641

so how do we do it?

breaking bread

Grace is a good place to start ... sing it, say a familiar prayer or make up your own!

use your musical gift

If you sing or play an instrument, share that with your lover. Or pop in a praise CD as you work around the house.

reading scripture

It's as easy as picking up a Bible! You could begin by reading the New Testament a few paragraphs at a time, then discussing and praying together over what you felt and discovered about Jesus and His disciples.

as you prepare for your wedding

In the video, Fr. Jeff Vomund suggested reading together the choices of wedding Scriptures. Then talk about the thoughts and feelings that come up from your reading. For example: You might ask God's blessings on your life and for the safety of friends and family who will travel to your wedding; ask for peace and that things will go smoothly during the days before your wedding. Close by saying an Our Father or another familiar prayer.

daily reflections

One really easy way to connect in prayer is to pick up a daily reflection booklet at your Christian bookstore, local church or online. These are usually one-page reflections with a scripture reading, a commentary and a prayer.

just talk to God, like you would talk to a friend!

"For where two or three are gathered in my name, there am I in the midst of them." Matt 18:20

As you two begin a discussion, God is already present with you, but in calling upon God's name, you bring to consciousness the reality. Then just BE REAL, totally yourself. Explore thoughts and feelings, values and needs. Spend some time in silence, listening. God will often speak to us through our spouse or in the silence. In leaving our questions and needs with God we will experience a peace that passes understanding.

gratitude and requests journal

All you need is a small blank book and pen! For each day, turn to a fresh page and on one side of the fold write five things for which you are grateful that day (this can be anything from the sunny day to the old car starting right up). On the other side of the fold, write your requests to God (health, children, the courage to ask for a raise at work, etc.). Do this every-day and you will be able to look back to see your prayers answered and an abundance of blessings! You're keeping a record of how God has worked in your life.

DTR with GOD

Just as the Daily Temperature Reading is an easy tool for free-flowing communication between spouses, it can be adapted for communicating with God, as well. Unlike the DTR you do with your spouse, you won't get the verbal response from God, but do pause, during the process and afterwards to meditate and listen. While you may not hear a voice from the clouds, as you continue to pray God will speak to you, in your heart and through others.

Appreciation: Thanking God for the many blessings that have been bestowed upon you (your love for each other, your health, your family, etc.). This is a way of praising God.

New Information: While God is all-knowing, it never hurts to express your point of view on the things happening in your life. You can talk about the ways you see God acting in your life, new insights into your faith or give the news on friends and family.

Puzzles: Tell God what you wonder about. What are the mysteries in your life? Ask for answers, and listen for God's response in the coming days and weeks.

Complaint with Request for Change: Now, we aren't recommending that you ask for a change in God's behavior, that's not really feasible. However, you can tell God about a situation in your life that you don't much like and request God's help in making it better. For example, "God, I'm struggling with the situation at my office. I would prefer to work things out, but need help discerning the right way to go about it." Again, listening in your heart and watching for God acting through the people around you is critical.

Wishes, Hopes and Dreams: This is your chance to tell God what you want out of your life. Share the hopes you have for each other, for your children, for your friends, etc. Ask for good health, for protection, for happy times or whatever you desire, and have faith that God will provide what you truly need. (1)

You can indeed build a winning relationship when you invite God to be a companion on your marriage journey.

With appreciation to Virginia Satir

expressing yourself

The first step in improving communication skills is to be aware that communication encompasses not only the things you say (verbal communication), but also how you say it (tone of voice); as well as what you say with your facial expressions, gestures, touch and body language (non-verbal communication). In fact, the tone you use in speaking to others is often more important than what you say. The old adage "a picture is worth a thousand words" rings true with non-verbal communication. The verbal message is often lost or misconstrued when the non-verbal message says the opposite.

The best gift you can give your spouse is yourself. Revealing who you are means you share your thoughts, ideas, judgments, as well as your hopes, dreams and emotions. Personal, loving communication is essential for a healthy marriage. Feelings are neither right nor wrong. They are a part of who you are. It is your response to feelings that involves moral choices.

levels of communication

I	- Facts, details, information
II	- Ideas, thoughts, judgments
III	- Feelings, emotions, hopes, dreams. (intimate communication)

Notice that there are several LEVELS of expression. Most people have no trouble communicating on **Level I**. Giving your ideas, thoughts and judgments on **Level II** is more personal. However, **Level III** is the deepest most intimate communication you can achieve.

 Sometimes fear of being judged or misunderstood prevents us from sharing our feelings. How might this vulnerability keep you from revealing your feelings to your fiancé?

 Take a look at yourself. Do you try to convey your feelings mostly through facial expressions, body language, tone-of-voice or words? Think about a recent conflict you've had with your partner. How did you communicate most of your feelings (for example: eye rolling, smirking, hands on hips, crossed arms, sarcasm, etc.)?

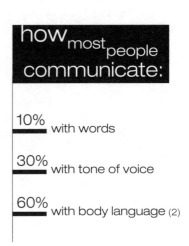

how most people communicate:

10% with words

30% with tone of voice

60% with body language (2)

14. ROADBLOCKS TO GOOD COMMUNICATION

Check any of the roadblocks to good communication that describe your behavior.

- ◯ Judging, criticizing, blaming
- ◯ Giving unsolicited advice
- ◯ Name calling, ridiculing
- ◯ Warning, threatening
- ◯ Ordering, commanding
- ◯ Preaching, moralizing
- ◯ Psychoanalyzing
- ◯ Withdrawing, refusing to talk
- ◯ Using sarcasm
- ◯ Shouting
- ◯ Can you think of any others

Star any roadblocks that describe your fiancé's behavior. Discuss responses with your fiancé.

15.

What positive communication skills did you experience in your family of origin?

- ◯ good listening
- ◯ sharing feelings
- ◯ affirming one another
- ◯ taking time to communicate
- ◯ good nonverbal messages
- ◯ respecting the other's opinion
- ◯ other

16.

Refer to the roadblocks from question 14. List some techniques that you witnessed being used in your family of origin.

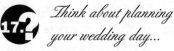

17. *Think about planning your wedding day...*

Circle 5 words from the list that describe some of the feelings you have had during this process. It is OK if these conflict.

Choose 2 to discuss with your fiancé.

Afraid
Amazed
Angry
Annoyed
Apprehensive
Appreciated
Bored
Carefree
Complacent
Confident
Confused
Disappointed
Disturbed
Ecstatic
Encouraged
Exhausted
Free
Friendly
Frustrated
Glad
Grateful
Happy
Helpless
Hopeless
Hurt
Inspired
Jealous
Lonely
Mellow
Nervous
Overwhelmed
Peaceful
Proud
Resentful
Sad
Secure
Surprised
Thankful
Troubled
Trusted
Unglued
Uptight
Upset
Worried

"I" vs "YOU" STATEMENTS

Speaking in "You" statements puts people on the defensive. "You" statements (e.g. *You made us late again; or You never help with the wedding plans*) end up blaming, judging or belittling the other person. "I" statements (e.g. *I feel embarrassed to arrive late; I feel overwhelmed with all the planning involved in our wedding.*) present observations, thoughts, feelings and wishes. "I" statements leave the other person open to responding.

Prayer of St. Francis

Lord, make me an instrument of Your peace.
Where there is hatred, let me sow love; where there
is injury, pardon; where there is doubt, faith; where
there is despair, hope; where there is darkness, light;
and where there is sadness, joy. O, Divine Master,
grant that I may not so much seek to be consoled
as to console; to be understood as to understand;
to be loved as to love; for it is in giving that we
receive; it is in pardoning that we are pardoned;
and it is in dying that we are born to eternal life.

Be conscious of the language you use.

This is a **vital piece** of skilled communication.

... and your eyes and your heart and your mind. Listening requires good eye contact and open body language. When you listen to the whole person, you listen for the feelings that are there and the meaning of their words. Only then are you truly listening with the intent to understand.

Experts say a person's greatest need is to be understood, to be affirmed, to be validated, and to be appreciated.(2) Isn't this what you want from the person you will marry, to know that your spouse understands who you are and appreciates and accepts you? Developing good listening skills with good communication skills can accomplish this for your marriage. **The highest level of listening is powerful, affirming and healing.**

HERE'S A TIP... | FOR BEING A GOOD LISTENER.

- **Have good eye contact and open body language.**

- **Watch for feelings and nonverbal messages.**

- **Give feedback: Rephrase the message and reflect the feelings.**

- **Ask questions.**

"The most important principle in the field of interpersonal relations is 'Seek first to understand, then to be understood.'"(2)

Stephen R. Covey

ASSESSING YOUR LISTENING SKILLS

 Check the column that best describes your behavior.

Assessing Good Listening Habits

	Often	Sometimes	Never
I rephrase my fiancé's point to check for understanding.	⎯⎯	⎯⎯	⎯⎯
I pay careful attention to body language and facial clues.	⎯⎯	⎯⎯	⎯⎯
I acknowledge what my fiancé is saying.	⎯⎯	⎯⎯	⎯⎯
I put myself in my fiancé's situation.	⎯⎯	⎯⎯	⎯⎯
I invite my fiancé to expand on his/her point.	⎯⎯	⎯⎯	⎯⎯
I ask my fiancé about his/her feelings on the topic.	⎯⎯	⎯⎯	⎯⎯
My facial expression and body language are open and inviting to him/her.	⎯⎯	⎯⎯	⎯⎯

Assessing Poor Listening Habits

My mind wanders when others are speaking.	⎯⎯	⎯⎯	⎯⎯
I tune out my fiancé to prepare my response.	⎯⎯	⎯⎯	⎯⎯
When I have strong feelings about something I cannot put them aside to really listen to my fiancé.	⎯⎯	⎯⎯	⎯⎯
I assume I know what my fiancé will say before I've heard it.	⎯⎯	⎯⎯	⎯⎯
I tend to finish his/her sentences.	⎯⎯	⎯⎯	⎯⎯
I correct insignificant facts or details.	⎯⎯	⎯⎯	⎯⎯
I focus on giving advice or solving a problem.	⎯⎯	⎯⎯	⎯⎯
I'm so anxious to tell my story or experience that I often monopolize the conversation.	⎯⎯	⎯⎯	⎯⎯
I react defensively and act impatiently.	⎯⎯	⎯⎯	⎯⎯

 Now that you've assessed your listening skills, what one area needs the most work?

 What one area would you most like your fiancé to work on in order to be a better listener?

conflict resolution

Learning how to deal constructively with anger and conflict situations is a skill that is important for a healthy, happy marriage.

21. When I am angry with someone, I:
✓ Check all that apply.

- [ ] use sarcasm
- [ ] use criticism, blame
- [ ] convey negative nonverbal messages
- [ ] use an unpleasant tone of voice
- [ ] walk away until I calm down
- [ ] hide my feelings
- [ ] other...

22. How do I normally handle conflict situations?

- [ ] ignore the conflict and pretend every thing is fine
- [ ] let the other person have their way (peace at any price)
- [ ] use an ultimatum to demand my way
- [ ] raise my voice and use profanity and criticism until the other person gives in
- [ ] ask the other person to discuss the problem and attempt to find a suitable solution/compromise
- [ ] tell a third person about the problem, instead of the person with whom I am angry.

23. Am I easily angered? ___ Yes ___ No

24. How would you rate your and your fiancé's ability to handle conflict situations?

___ excellent   ___ good   ___ fair   ___ poor

25. Is there a topic you are hesitant to discuss with your fiancé for fear of creating conflict?

How do you make a decision when you disagree?

○ you would decide

○ you would start a fight until you got your way

○ your fiancé would start a fight until he/she got his/her way

○ we don't - one of us gives the "silent treatment"

○ your fiancé would decide

○ you would compromise

 Name a topic about which you and your fiancé disagree.

 When conflict arises, it is a challenge to follow the Rules for Disagreements (page 75). These rules require good communication and listening skills and will enable you to put your relationship ahead of the issue at hand. When disagreements arise, do they usually result in:

○ my needs being met (I win - You lose)

○ my fiancé's needs being met (I lose - You win)

○ neither of our needs being met (I lose - You lose)

○ both of our needs being met (The relationship wins!)

Describe a major decision you have made together recently. How did you come to this decision? How did you feel about this decision afterwards? How do you think your fiancé felt about it?

As a result of your answers above, do you think you would benefit from anger management counseling?... From conflict management counseling? If yes to either question, are you willing to seek counseling? If not, why not?

Tear this out and hang on your refrigerator. You will have Rules for Disagreement and the DTR where they are easily accessible.

RULES FOR DISAGREEMENTS
(Refrigerator Copy)

1. Use "I" Statements and Avoid "You" Statements

I put you on the defensive if I start my sentence with "You…"

2. Use "Heart" Statements and Avoid "Head" Statements

I will tell you how I feel (not what I think). Please understand that my feelings are mine, that I have a right to them…and don't judge them.

3. Don't Interrupt

In this way, I will not only "hear" you, but I will truly "listen" to you and try to understand your view without rushing in with my own views. Then, please listen to me without interrupting.

4. Don't "De-personalize" the Fight

I will maintain eye contact with you. I will stop whatever else I am doing (like watching TV). I will not call you names, or trivialize your view by making a "joke" out of it. I will sit down with you and talk it through. I won't walk out, unless we both agree to cool down for awhile. Please treat me with the same respect.

5. Fight Lovingly

I understand that "fighting" and "loving" are not necessarily different. Even in my anger and rage, I love you. I promise that even in the midst of our fighting, I will not say or do anything that will belittle or destroy you or our relationship. Please deal with me and our relationship in the same nurturing way.

6. Keep It Simple

I will try as hard as possible to be clear and stick to the issue at hand. Because I may be emotional, angry, or hurting, it may be difficult for me to talk. But I promise to try. If nothing else, I will tell you, "I feel angry" or "I feel hurt." I ask you to also be clear and to not bring up past issues.

7. Don't Play Mind Games

I will always try to be direct and sincere with you; I will not play games or fool with the "trust" and "honesty" that our relationship is built on. I ask that you try to be direct with me too, avoiding any mental or emotional games.

8. Don't Abuse

I realize that I know things about you that no one else knows. I know what topics are sensitive to you. I know your weak spots. I promise not to abuse this almost-sacred knowledge I have. I promise not to abuse you. I ask that you not abuse me, for I too am vulnerable to you.

9. Don't Be Afraid to Seek Professional Help

If our fighting happens more often and increases in its intensity and we feel that our differences are becoming unmanageable, then let's contact a counselor. I realize that we may feel foolish, embarrassed, or unsure as we seek this help. But I also realize it's better to err on the side of caution than to watch our marriage die.

On the video you witnessed Susan Edwards teaching the Daily Temperature Reading to a young couple and practicing it with her husband, Bob. The DTR is one of many relationship skills offered by PAIRS. To get more information on all the skills in the PAIRS "tool box" please see the Resource section in the back of this book. Practicing the Daily Temperature Reading is an excellent way to create a habit that will keep your focus on the need for open and effective communication.

How to ask a spouse to do a DTR:

■ Ask your spouse if they will do a DTR with you and give them a time limit (usually 5-8 minutes).

■ If it is a good time for the DTR, sit in a position that is comfortable. Make every attempt to give good eye contact and to touch your spouse (such as a position of knee-to-knee or hand-to-hand).

■ Remember to listen carefully to your partner and say "thank you" after their statements.

■ First, the one who initiated the DTR gives an appreciation. The spouse says "thank you" and then gives an appreciation.

■ If something comes up that needs a longer discussion, agree to set time aside later. Do not exceed your agreed upon time for this DTR.

■ If, when you ask your spouse to do a DTR, they say it is not a good time for them, perhaps you could agree to a time when it will be convenient.

---

the **D**aily **T**emperature **R**eading

▶ Appreciation

▶ New Information

▶ Puzzles

▶ Complaints With Request for Change

▶ Wishes, Hopes and Dreams

With appreciation to Virginia Satir

Confiding – the ability to reveal yourself fully, honestly and directly to another human being is the lifeblood of intimacy.

It's frightening to be in a close relationship in which silences, hidden agendas, contradictions and inconsistencies are a steady diet. No matter how much in love two people are or how well suited to each other, no relationship can flourish under that kind of strain. **Clear, regular communication is needed to live and work together with satisfaction.**

In relationships that go well, couples tend to maintain an easy, flowing communication about the big and little things that are going on in their lives. On the basis of this observation, Virginia Satir developed a technique for keeping each other up-to-date, which she called the Daily Temperature Reading (DTR). This simple technique has become a major source of relationship pleasure for many couples. It also works well in other settings and in other relationships.

Practical

Application of

Intimate

Relationship

Skills

PAIRS graduates tell me [Dr. Lori Gordon] two things about the Daily Temperature Reading: that it is one of the most important techniques they have for staying close and that all too often, when they get busy, they let it slide.

Don't let it slide!

Take a Temperature Reading on each other once a day. This is an important way to maintain or develop open, flowing communication in your relationship. You will evolve your own style for doing it, but here's the basic format you will want to work from.

step 1
appreciation

We need to be told what's good about us, and nobody is better equipped to tell us than the person who is closest to us. We hear much about what's wrong with us, both from the world at large and from ourselves (usually we are our own worst critics). When you see something in your partner that you appreciate, express it – either with words or with a gesture, but express it. Many of us also have to learn to accept our partner's appreciation. Often we have a conditioned response of brushing off compliments ("Oh, this old thing?" or "It was nothing"). We need to accept what they say and to thank them for saying it.

step 2
new information

When we fail to provide routine information about what's going on with us, there's too much room left for making assumptions. Intimacy thrives only when partners know what is happening in each other's lives - the trivial as well as the important. It may be related to work ("I finally got that new contract"), family,("my sister is having a baby"), mutual concerns and interests ("I'm worried about that mole on your neck" or "Here's an article I think you'd enjoy reading") or friends ("I had lunch with...") whatever it takes to keep contact alive and let your partner in on your moods, states, experiences – your life. Many problems and misunderstandings arise because we make assumptions about what's going on with our partner, since no one is providing actual information.

step 3
puzzles

If there are things you don't understand (why your partner seemed so down last night, the latest news about the office reorganization, why Mary and Pete broke up) and your partner can explain, ask. Don't assume that your partner knows that you are interested. Not asking might well be seen as indifference. Some believe, "If you wanted to know, you would ask me." Others think, "If you wanted me to know, you would tell me." Thus do many puzzles go unresolved and questions unanswered – a ripe situation for assumptions and mind reading to develop. If there are things you don't understand that your partner could help clarify, ask for clarification.

This is also an opportunity to explore and voice any puzzling questions you may have about yourself. ("I'm really far behind on that project at work and I don't understand why I can't sit down and get it done. I seem to have a real block." "I'm really not sure why I got so angry last night while we were trying to balance the checkbook." "Somebody snapped my head off at work over something minor and it really upset me. I don't know why it bothered me so much, since it was a small thing and something obviously was bothering me.") Bringing up such personal quandaries doesn't mean you will suddenly find answers, but discussing them can give your partner more insight about your conflicts and thoughts.

step 4 complaints with request for change

These need not be blaming or judgmental. Simply say, "This thing happened that bothered me, and I would feel better if you did this other thing instead." When you state your complaint, **be specific** about the behavior that bothers you and state the **behavior** you are asking for instead. All too often, we subject people to long lists of "don't do this" and "don't do that" without ever telling them what **we do want**. Yelling, "Why don't you ever come home on time?" won't get the same response as "If you're going to

recommended sentence stems
"I notice…" & "I would prefer…"

be late, please call. That way I can make my own plans and I won't worry about you." If emotional or touchy issues come up that need long discussion, you might want to set aside a more appropriate time to deal with them in depth.

The Daily Temperature Reading is intended to provide information. It is not intended to serve as a serious conflict-resolving tool – its purpose is to help prevent misunderstandings. If you're interested in deeper conflict resolution skills, PAIRS provides a variety of methods to prevent touchy issues from erupting into full-scale battles in which you drag every grudge you've ever had into play.

step 5 wishes, hopes and dreams

Our hopes and dreams are integral, vital parts of who and what we are. If we don't share them with our partner, we are depriving him or her of an important part of ourselves. In a world where much of our time is spent reacting to various immediate pressures, we rarely have time to think beyond the moment. This part of the DTR gives us a chance to reflect on what **we** want – from ourselves, from our partners and from life. The more we can bring our expectations and hopes into our own and our partner's awareness, the more likely it is that we'll find a way to realize them. They can extend from the mundane to the grandiose: "I hope you can get this weekend shift off so we can spend more time together." "I hope we can have a baby." "I wish that someday we could have a house in the country." "I dream of having the time to leave for a month and go hiking in Alaska." "I wish I had time to concentrate on my painting."

It may seem awkward and artificial to do the DTR at first. Don't let that prevent you from using it. As you become accustomed to it, you will find yourself touching on most areas automatically. You won't always have something to say in all five categories each day, but I encourage you to set aside a brief period of time every day to give yourself the opportunity to think about each area. *Appreciations nurture the relationship, New Information, Puzzles and Complaints prevent misunderstanding and solve problems, and Wishes, Hopes and Dreams offer a future to look forward to.*

Some people who take the PAIRS course initially resist this idea because it seems to run counter to the spontaneity they want in their relationship. But they have found that if they stick with it the structure gives way to real sharing and allows just the spark of spontaneity they are seeking. Many people are surprised to discover that when they think about it, their day at work wasn't as boring as they believed, or that it is easier than they thought to be both direct and kind when they tell somebody they love that they are doing something annoying or irritating – and they get results. If you did not give yourself time to be fanciful and to share fantasies with your partner, you may never have discovered that you both dreamed about opening a bed and breakfast and that maybe you will be able to pull together the resources to give it a shot.(4)

" ... How wonderful the bond between two believers, now one in hope, one in desire, one in discipline, one in the same service! They are both children of one Father and servants of the same Master, undivided in spirit and flesh, truly two in one flesh. "

Tertullian, Ad uxorem as cited in the
Catechism of the Catholic Church #1642

Communication with each other and God is the foundation for a winning relationship!

Chapter 5:

COMMUNICATION

STEWARDSHIP AND YOUR

Chapter 6:

FINANCE$

FOR RICHER OR
FOR POORER

Our culture sends us loud and clear messages about money and possessions. Advertisers bombard us with messages that tell us how to have worth, how to look and how using their product will make us sexy and desirable. Listen carefully and you will realize that you will never have "enough."

Christians look at the bigger picture and have a very different perspective. We see God as our generous creator and giver of all our gifts. Because of God's blessings we have the ability to support ourselves. Since all that we have comes from God and belongs to God, we are merely **"stewards"** or caretakers of God's gifts - our **time**, our **talent** and our **treasure** - while here on earth. Thinking this way affects the way we live, changes our values and influences the way we set goals and priorities. Money becomes just a tool to bring about your hopes, dreams and plans for your life, and your time and talent become part of the gift you give back to family, church and community.

a look at time and talent

This is a finance chapter but before we look at treasure, we want to first look at other areas of stewardship. Your **time** is a very valuable and precious resource. Many people put off doing charitable things until they "have more time." The fact is we will always have ways to fill our time. Until we set priorities and make the decision to give of our time to God and pray about what God is calling us to do, we may never find that time to give to others.

 What is one way to share your time with your parish, community or other charity? (i.e. An hour mentoring a child, an hour with an elderly person in a nursing home, etc.)

Each person is created with special **talents**. Many skills are developed in school or your job. Be creative about how you can turn your talent into an opportunity to help your community, parish or school.

 Give examples of how you have used your talents in the past to help others. What one talent could you use to enrich your parish or community? (i.e. volunteer to help a Girl Scout project, offer carpentry skills at parish, etc.)

your family of origin and the bigger picture

 How was your family active in sharing their talents and giving their time to support church or community activities and programs?

 Did your family of origin go the extra mile and sacrifice something of themselves to help other people?

5. Did your parents contribute financially to their church and/or other charities?

 6. How do you think your family of origin's example will influence you to share your time, talent and treasure with your church and community?

"For where your treasure is, there also will your heart be."

Matthew 6:21

 7. What attitudes or expectations about money matters were a part of your family of origin?

 Check all that apply.

____ The person making the most money should decide how it is spent.

____ The husband is the primary breadwinner.

____ The amount of money a person earns is a measure of his/her worth.

____ The wife is responsible for paying the bills and controlling the money.

____ A budget is not necessary.

____ How can I be out of money when I still have checks?

____ It is important to have an emergency fund for such things as medical bills, car repairs, appliance breakdowns, etc.

____ Two incomes are necessary to achieve an expected lifestyle.

____ It's important to know the difference between wants and needs.

____ Living from paycheck to paycheck is okay.

____ Saving money and budgeting are very important in order to be financially secure.

____ Competing with neighbors and others to own the biggest and best is important.

____ It is not important to contribute to the Church.

____ The couple needs to discuss financial issues and plan for the future.

____ The husband is responsible for paying the bills and controlling the money.

____ Credit Card debt is a necessity.

____ A budget is important.

____ No need to plan for the future. The future will take care of itself.

____ Saving money is not important.

____ There is no need to balance a checkbook.

____ It is important to contribute to the Church.

____ The couple should not talk about money matters because it is unpleasant and may lead to conflict.

____ Other _____

 Go back and "star" those statements that describe YOUR attitudes and expectations.

8. What one attitude/expectation most surprised you in question 7?

 9. Name one or two attitudes/expectations of yours which will be helpful for handling finances in your marriage.

 10. Name one or two attitudes/expectations of yours which may lead to problems in your marriage.

> Good stewards realize the difference between owning possessions and being owned by their possessions. If you need all of your time, talent and treasure just to maintain an impressive home, then you are not leaving much room in life for anything else.

attitudes and expectations

 11. Describe your personal needs and wishes for the first five years of marriage regarding the quality and cost of:

✽ Your apartment/home (modest vs. mansion)

✽ The car you drive (Lexus vs. Chevy; used vs. new)

✽ The clothes you wear (Saks vs. Target)

✽ The restaurants you frequent (five star vs. fast food)

✽ Jewelry (diamonds vs. costume)

✽ Vacations (cruise vs. camping)

✽ Hobbies/Interests (boating, gambling, bowling, season tickets)

✽ Home electronics (big screen TV, latest computer, DVD, cell phones, etc.)

12.? Do you believe your needs and wishes identified in question 11 will allow/require you to live

_____ below your level of income? _____ at your level of income? _____ above your level of income?

? Who do you expect will earn the money on which you will live?
_____ husband _____ wife _____ both

? What about after children?
_____ husband _____ wife _____ both

? Do you think your fiancé agrees with your answers?

13.? What level of income do you believe is necessary...
at the time you are married? _____
after one year of marriage? _____
after five years of marriage? _____

14.? Are you willing to lower your lifestyle expectations if things do not work out as planned? Explain your answer.

15.? How much money do you think you should be able to spend without consulting your spouse?

16.? In what areas of your life would you consider borrowing money?
✓ Check all that apply.
○ education
○ vacations
○ groceries
○ entertainment activities
○ car
○ home
○ clothes
○ jewelry
○ other_____

? Do you believe your fiancé agrees with you?

#1 PROBLEM IN MARRIAGE: **LACK OF COMMUNICATION**

#1 ISSUE NOT DISCUSSED: **MONEY**

#1 CRISIS IN MARRIAGE: **DEBT**

These statistics are reflected in the survey responses at the Center for Marriage and Family at Creighton University (2000)(1) in which finances was one of the top three obstacles for couples in the first five years of marriage. The financial problem areas mentioned included:

▶ **DEBT BROUGHT INTO THE MARRIAGE**

▶ **SPENDING HABITS IN PRESENT FINANCIAL SITUATION**

▶ **FINANCIAL DECISION-MAKING**

▶ **EMPLOYMENT OF SPOUSES**

Couples who have a healthy, open line of communication will have the least problems based on money. That's because the conflict regarding money issues is not caused by how much money you have, but rather diverse attitudes, expectations, goals and values regarding money issues.

sharing a vision

Couples who divide their money into HIS, HERS and OURS communicate unspoken messages. Sometimes this division of money implies a lack of unity and trust for one another. Sometimes couples do not even know what the other is earning or spending. If there is a selfish quality to the arrangement it could indicate a lack of total commitment to the marriage. Husbands and wives who **share joint accounts** and communicate about expenses and incomes **demonstrate trust, unity and respect** for one another.

 Does your fiancé know how much money you make? ... how much you have saved? how much debt you carry?

 Do you know how much money your fiancé earns? ... how much he/she has saved? how much debt he/she carries?

 Have you discussed career goals and the impact they will have on time spent with family, earning potential and relocation issues?

 Have you ever discussed how you would feel about being transferred or moving to another city?

21. Evaluate your spending/saving habits.
✓ Check all that apply.

_____ I regularly allocate a portion of my income to savings.

_____ I live from paycheck to paycheck.

_____ I have a lot of credit card debt and loans.

_____ I own more clothes than I could possibly wear.

_____ I buy items that I never use.

_____ I have no idea where all my money goes from each paycheck.

_____ I keep track of all my expenses and know exactly how I spend my money.

_____ I put off buying something when I don't have the cash for it.

_____ I never thought about the distinction between a need and a want regarding my purchases.

22. Would you describe yourself as a saver or a spender? Would you describe your fiancé as a saver or a spender? Give one example illustrating your answer.

23. What underlying negative attitudes may be attached to money matters for you?
✓ Check all that apply.

_____ When I feel lonely or frustrated I go on a shopping spree.

_____ Buying new clothes or other items makes me feel good about myself.

_____ I sometimes feel embarrassed to make less than my friends.

_____ It makes me feel important to pick up the bar or meal tab for a group of friends.

_____ I like to show off the new things I buy. I feel like people admire my success.

_____ I tell everyone how much I make in order to impress them.

_____ I'm so afraid of being destitute that I want to hoard my money for a rainy day.

_____ Money is more valuable to me than friendships.

_____ I feel reluctant to share my money because I worked hard to earn it.

_____ I'm afraid to make a budget because I will fail to keep it.

_____ I feel anxious about sharing a bank account with my fiancé because we have such
different spending/saving habits.

_____ I need the freedom and independence to spend my money as I want.

_____ I can't be happy unless I have a certain income and lifestyle.

_____ Other _____

24. What one item above surprised you?

Do you suspect that any of your previous answers could become significant problems in your marriage?

 Do you have any debts or ongoing expenses that will carry over into your marriage? What are they?

 If you are bringing debt into your marriage, do you feel embarrassed or reluctant to discuss it with your fiancé?

 If one person is bringing debt into the marriage, are you willing to work out a plan together to get out of debt that may include:
✓ Check all that apply.

____ deferring purchases of a home, car, furniture, etc. until debt is paid off

____ cutting up your credit cards

____ cutting back on unnecessary expenses (e.g. travel, entertainment, clothing)

____ going to Consumer Debt Counseling or other professionals for assistance

____ other _____

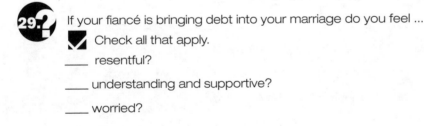 If your fiancé is bringing debt into your marriage do you feel ...
✓ Check all that apply.
____ resentful?

____ understanding and supportive?

____ worried?

____ other _____

 Are you willing to plan a budget with your fiancé?

 Do you have the discipline required to live within your budget?

a way of life

As you read at the beginning of this chapter, the way a Christian couple looks at their resources is a much bigger picture than just their financial assets. Along with treasure, they take into consideration their time and talent and view all as a gift from God. Gratitude for these gifts leads to a desire to give back.

In the Hebrew Scriptures, God asked the Israelites to tithe - to give the first 10% back to God. In the Christian Scriptures, Jesus taught us to serve others, to use our talents and to give to God what is God's. **Many Catholics tithe 10% of their gross income, with 5% going to their parish and 5% to other charities.** We all have a responsibility to share our financial income. The decision that you and your spouse will make should result in a feeling of peace in your hearts and a sense of joy in your giving. The decision of what is right for you is between you and God.

In the video, the Naville's talked about their tithing. In the beginning it was an "obligation," but soon became a joyful way of life. That "way of life" was just a part of being a Christian. You may not imagine yourself giving 10% of your income to the church and charities right now, but it is a goal to set and aim towards. There are several reasons tithing benefits YOU.

- You are not "attached" to your possessions. You become free.
- A part of everything you receive flows through you to others and helps the needy.
- God promises that if you are faithful to His will, He will be faithful.

"Give and gifts will be given to you: a good measure, packed together, shaken down and overflowing, will be poured into your lap. For the measure with which you measure will in return be measured out to you."

Luke 6:38

 What did you learn about the value of tithing?

 What are some charities you would like to support in the early years of your marriage?
Are you willing to pray about tithing as a part of giving your time, talent and treasure back to God?

Prenuptial Agreements put up a red flag for first marriages. These financial contracts can imply a "yours and mine" attitude, a lack of unity and trust. Protecting YOUR assets can indicate a lack of commitment in the marriage and a materialistic, selfish attitude.

 If you have plans to enter into a Prenuptial Agreement, explain how this is life-giving and healthy for your marriage.

HERE'S A TIP Three Keys to Money Management

1. Size up current situation - income, savings, debt, potential.
2. Formulate a cost of living plan - expenses (Don't outspend your income).
3. Identify short term and long term goals. (2)

You have looked at the bigger picture and answered questions about your attitudes and expectations for Time, Talent and Treasure in your marriage. Because The Center for Marriage and Family tells us in their 2000 survey that lack of communication about money is the number one crisis in families,(3) Consumer Debt Counseling of St. Louis is providing you with The Newlyweds' Guide to Money Management. You will find this guide in the back of your workbook. This is the most comprehensive, helpful guide that we can provide. Please use this to communicate about your money, to plan your budget and to set short and long term goals.

"No one can receive anything except what has been given him from heaven."

John 3:27

**Christ has no body now on earth but yours;
no hands but yours, no feet but yours.
Yours are the eyes through which
He is to go about doing good;
yours are the hands with which
He is to bless people now.**

St. Teresa of Avila

$ Money
is only a tool.

Strive together to be excellent stewards of all your resources.

STEWARDSHIP
AND YOUR
Chapter 6: FINANCE$

Chapter 7: PLANNING AND PARENTING OF CHILDREN

WILL YOU ACCEPT CHILDREN LOVINGLY FROM GOD

> ❝Children are the supreme gift of marriage and contribute greatly to the good of the parents themselves.❞
>
> *Gaudium et Spes* 50.1 (1)

Having a baby is one of the most joyful experiences for a married couple. Have you and your fiancé prayed about, discussed and agreed upon the major issues that pertain to starting a family? These include **when to have children, how many children to have, openness to God's will and the method you will use for the planning and spacing of children.** Anything short of full agreement may result in feelings of resentment that will eventually affect not only your sexual relationship, but all aspects of your couple relationship.

Children change your life. The husband and wife go from being a couple to becoming a family. Parents take on the responsibility of nurturing, loving and disciplining their children. There are many sacrifices, but also many rewards in becoming parents. Considerations include the impact on jobs and careers, the quality and cost of care-takers, the type and cost of education and a generous review of priorities. In becoming co-creators with God, parents take on a commitment to accept their children and to participate with God in educating and raising them to be responsible, spiritual and moral individuals.

> " Parents are the principal and first educators of their children.(Cf. GE 3.)
> In this sense the fundamental task of marriage and family is to be at the service of life.(Cf. FC 28.) "
>
> *Catechism of the Catholic Church #1653*

becoming parents

 1. How many children do you hope to have? Why this number?

 2. How long do you want to wait after marriage to have a baby? Why?

3. What are some reasons you want to have children?

____ It's expected.   ____ I want a baby to love me and whom I can love.

____ Babies are so cute.   ____ My parents want to be grandparents.

____ My biological clock is ticking.   ____ I want to stay at home and not work.

____ We have so much love to share.   ____ We want to nurture, love and raise children.

____ It will strengthen our marriage.   ____ Other _____

4. If you find yourselves facing infertility, to what extent and expense will you go in order to have your own biological child?

 5. How do you feel about adoption?

 6. If you had an unplanned pregnancy, how would you react? How do you think your spouse would react?

 7. How would you respond if your child was born with mental or physical disabilities? How do you think your spouse would respond?

raising children

" Children are a gift from the LORD."
Psalm 127 : 3

 8. What are three positive, healthy aspects about how you were raised?

9. What are three negative, unhealthy aspects about how you were raised?

 10. Are you willing to consider taking parenting classes in order to learn positive parenting skills?

 11. If you had the choice between both of you being employed or one working outside the home, with the other staying home to care for your children, which would you choose? Why?

JUST REMEMBER

Our own parents are our most powerful teachers about how to raise children.

12. If you hope to have one parent stay at home with the children, whom do you expect to take on this role?

13. Who will be the preferred primary care-giver of your children if both of you work outside the home?

____ day care   ____ nanny   ____ neighbor/friend   ____ grandparent   ____ other_____

14. What type of education would you prefer for your children?

____ public school   ____ private or parochial school   ____ home-schooling

JUST REMEMBER

The answers you give to the questions in this book are merely a snapshot of your opinions, thoughts and feelings, right now. It is very important to continually re-evaluate your feelings on all the issues raised in this program. For example, on the video you just watched, Teresa Kahre said she had always envisioned herself continuing to work in public relations, however when her first child was born, she began to feel that she should give up that career to stay at home with her daughter. Teresa had to be **open to change, willing to listen** to what her heart was saying and to **pray for help** in making the right choice. It is clear from her statements that though she and Jim had to make some sacrifices and tough choices, they have an overwhelming sense of joy in their situation. So remember, be on the lookout for changes in your attitudes, opinions and ways of thinking about all aspects of your marriage. Be open to growth and change in both of your outlooks, discuss it together and ask God for guidance and help in making your decisions.

15. Check the statements with which you agree. Discuss your answers.

____ Both husband and wife need to be involved in disciplining the children.

____ It's primarily the mother's responsibility to care for the children.

____ Physical punishment (e.g. spanking) is necessary.

____ A child needs to feel loved and accepted.

____ Parents need to limit their child's activity schedule.

____ Vacations should always include the children.

____ Children need to be respected.

____ The children's needs always come before the husband and wife's relationship.

You're Always a Couple...

During the early years of your children's lives, it may seem like every moment is consumed by caring for their needs. To a great extent this is very true. Obviously, babies and toddlers need nearly constant attention and care. Because of this, it can be all too easy to let your couple relationship suffer. Eventually it may seem that all you communicate about is the children. Even worse, some couples use the children's needs and lives to avoid talking about their own issues. No one is suggesting you neglect your children, but rather encouraging you to be careful to nurture the bond you have as a couple. The most important relationship in the household is that of the parents. After all, if the parents don't maintain a strong, healthy marriage, the children suffer. Be creative about ways to keep your marriage vital after children. Plan regular "dates," be romantic, give it that extra bit of energy after long days. If you do, you'll have a happier, more satisfying life together and your kids will have a wonderful example to follow.

planning and spacing of children

The Catholic Church teaches that by God's design, sexual love possesses a life-giving nature. This life-giving nature is intentionally separated from the act of intercourse by use of artificial contraceptives. Contraception destroys the full meaning of sexual love as intended by God.

While artificial methods of birth control may be very popular, they eliminate God from the covenant marriage relationship, destroy the full meaning of marital intercourse, do not encourage the benefits of periodic abstinence and pose many side effects and health risks. In using Natural Family Planning (NFP), the couple places no barriers between themselves and no potentially harmful chemicals in the woman's body. The truth is that the only method that protects the natural connection between life and love is natural family planning. That is why the Catholic Church embraces **only** natural forms of family planning. NFP respects the integrity of men and women and is supportive to the marriage covenant. The couple partners with God, as co-creators of new life.

A couple should be responsible in planning their family. After prayerful consideration, couples may decide to space their children for the good of one another and to provide for all the needs of the family. This decision is not made lightly, but unselfishly and with an openness to God's plan. Make a decision as a couple that will have a positive effect on your marriage relationship.

> **❝** To experience the gift of married love while respecting the laws of conception is to acknowledge that one is not the **master** of the sources of life, but rather the **minister** of the design established by the Creator. **❞**
>
> *Humanae Vitae* 13 (2)

 16.2 Review your beliefs and impressions of Natural Family Planning (NFP) by answering these questions.

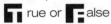 **T**rue or **F**alse

____ NFP offers several models and styles for naturally planning and spacing children.

____ Periodic abstinence from sexual relations will not hurt our marriage, but strengthen it.

____ Family planning methods are the responsibility of both the husband and wife.

____ Today's methods of Natural Family Planning are more effective than condoms.

____ Today's methods of Natural Family Planning are as effective as birth control pills.

____ NFP has no side effects that can threaten the man or woman's health.

____ NFP can be used to avoid or achieve a pregnancy.

____ NFP is very helpful in resolving fertility problems.

____ Sex becomes more meaningful for most couples using NFP.

____ God calls married couples to be open to creating new life.

____ A man is fertile every day of the month.

____ A woman is fertile only a limited number of days each month.

____ NFP is morally acceptable to people of all faiths.

The correct answer to each of the above is TRUE.

Advantages of NFP are reflected in some of the comments from couples in the video:

"There's a **peace** in knowing we are doing what **God** wants."

"Periods of **abstinence** have become **courtship opportunities**."

"**Sex** becomes more meaningful. **NFP** helps keep our **passion alive**."

"There are **NO WARNING LABELS** on **NFP**."

WHAT EXACTLY IS NATURAL FAMILY PLANNING?

Natural Family Planning (NFP) is a system of understanding a couple's combined fertility through observation of natural changes in the woman's body. Couples may then record this information to avoid or achieve pregnancy naturally, without using drugs, surgery or devices. This information also gives insight into a woman's reproductive health. Couples use this method together, creating good communication between them, which promotes a stronger, healthier relationship.

How does it work? Barring any medical problems, men are always fertile. On the other hand, women alternate between periods of fertility and infertility. By cooperating with this cycle, couples can effectively achieve or avoid pregnancy.

During an introductory session with a qualified instructor, the couple will learn the different signs that the woman may observe throughout her cycle and how to record them. Around the time of ovulation, the hormone estrogen rises, causing mucus inside the women's cervix to change. External observation of this type of mucus indicates that the woman has entered the brief, fertile part of her cycle. Additionally, changes in the cervix and woman's body temperature may be observed. After ovulation, the hormone progesterone changes the mucus in such a way that it is obvious that the time of fertility has passed. The couple, with proper instruction, can use this information to plan their family.

If couples wish to avoid pregnancy, they abstain from genital contact during the time of fertility. If couples wish to conceive a baby, they plan intercourse during the time of fertility. In order to use Natural Family Planning effectively, it is necessary to receive instruction from a qualified provider. It is not within the scope of this marriage preparation program to teach NFP. Classes are offered to assist couples in understanding the scientific basis of NFP, the practicalities of using it and the rewards it will foster in their relationship. Modern methods of NFP are 97-99.5% effective to avoid pregnancy when taught and used correctly. They are also very effective to achieve pregnancy when fertile days are identified and used for intercourse.(3)

NaProTECHNOLOGY is a new reproductive science that partners with the Creighton Model of natural fertility care. It assists couples who find themselves infertile, as well as women with hormonal disorders (including PMS!!) and other fertility related issues. An amazing fact is that NaPro Technology is 72% effective in helping couples with infertility achieve a pregnancy.(4)

SPICE

I feel loved...

S piritually, when...

P hysically, when...

I ntellectually, when...

C ommunicatively, when...

E motionally, when...

There are many times in a marriage where couples find it necessary to avoid genital contact. Besides the routine events of family life, work and day to day life, there are occasions when a spouse is traveling, ill, stressed or simply involved in other things. Couples who use a natural form of family planning and want to avoid a pregnancy, avoid genital contact on the identified days of fertility in the cycle. This can be a time of great intimacy for the couple. This intimacy is "sexual" in the true sense of the word, embracing all we are as men and women. An acronym to describe this multi-dimensional view of sexuality is S-P-I-C-E.

S piritual ... expressed through praying together or meditation.

P hysical ... expressed through touching and holding one another.

I ntellectual ... expressed through sharing a project, book or new learning.

C reative/**C** ommunicative ... expressed through an increase in written or verbal communication or other shared activities.

E motional ... expressed through sharing feelings, desires and humor.

Men and women relate to one another in all of these ways throughout their lives. Couples using NFP to plan their families are in an ideal situation to further develop these areas of SPICE, especially during periods of abstinence, an opportunity not encouraged by artificial birth control methods. Couples can develop SPICE lists (see left) for one another to express their desires in all of these areas. They are often surprised at the increased intimacy and marital bonding they experience through this process. Natural forms of family planning invite a sprinkling of SPICE into the relationship. Take this opportunity to create a SPICE list! (4)

Natural Family Planning   vs   Artificial Birth Control

Natural Family Planning	Artificial Birth Control
• Promotes marital bonding.	• May promote feelings of being used.
• Reports less than 5% divorce rate.	• Reports greater than 50% divorce rate.
• Is open to God's will for life.	• Is closed to beginning a new life.
• Is safe, reliable, and scientific.	• Has many health risks; some methods have low effectiveness.
• Fosters communication.	• Requires little/no communication.
• Treats fertility as a gift.	• Treats fertility as a disease.
• Is effective to avoid or achieve pregnancy.	• Use only to avoid pregnancy.
• Encourages SPICE.	• Discourages SPICE.
• Is in harmony with fertility.	• Interferes with fertility.
• Supports the nature and meaning of marriage as intended by God.	• Interferes with the nature and meaning of marriage as intended by God.

 What about NFP especially appeals to you?

 What about NFP concerns you?

 What about artificial contraception concerns you?

 How do you feel about using Natural Family Planning in your marriage?

"The church ... teaches that each and every marital act must of necessity retain its intrinsic relationship to the procreation of human life."

Humanae Vitae, 11 (5)

step-parenting

Step-parenting is one of the single most difficult challenges for married couples. Problems between spouses concerning step-children cause the break-up of many marriages. Although this marriage preparation program cannot deal with step-parenting in great detail, the following are questions intended to help you communicate about your present feelings, hopes and desires about creating your new family.

If your fiancé has a child(ren):

 21. How do you feel about his/her child(ren)? How do you think the child(ren) feel about you? About your marriage? Why?

 22. Do you think the child(ren)'s feelings or your feelings will be a help or a hindrance to building a strong family unit? Explain your answer.

 23. What concerns do you have about taking on the responsibility of being a step-parent?

 24. How do you feel about the legal agreements made for the care of the child?

 25. How do you feel about the child support financial agreement and the impact that will have on your marriage?

 26. How much time will you spend alone with the step-children? How will you spend it?

If you have child(ren) from a previous relationship:

 27. How do you think your fiancé feels about your child(ren)?

 28. How do you think the child(ren) feel about your fiancé? About your marriage? Why?

 29. Do you think the child(ren)'s feelings or your fiancé's feelings will be a help or hindrance to building a strong family unit? Explain your answer.

 30. Do you have concerns about your fiancé taking on the responsibility of being a step-parent?

 31. How do you think your fiancé feels about the legal agreements made for the care of the child?

 32. How do you think your fiancé feels about the child support financial agreement and the impact that will have on your marriage?

 33. How much time will you spend alone with your child(ren)?

About your newly formed family:

 34. Do you anticipate problems in disciplining the child(ren)? Explain.

 35. Will the child(ren) accept the authority of the new step-parent? Explain.

 36. Have you agreed on the roles each of you will play as parent/step-parent? What are they?

 37. When step-children visit, will they be treated as guests or as "family?"

 38. If you do not have primary custody, how often do you expect the child(ren) to be with you?

 39. How will you balance your couple needs with the needs of the step-children when they visit?

 40. Would it be wise to get family counseling before your marriage?

 41. Are you willing to get counseling if either you, your fiancé or the child(ren) appear to have some adjustment problems with the new marriage? If not, why not?

A step-family is born of many losses.

Family members have different
histories and expectations.

Parent-child relationships predate
the relationship of the new couple.

An influential biological parent exists elsewhere
in actuality or in memory.

Children may be members of
two or more households.

Ann Getzoff and Carolyn McClenahan *Step-kids: A survival Guide for Teenagers in Step-families.* (6)

When you welcome children into your family you become co-creators with God.

Chapter 8:

I PROMISE TO LOVE YOU AND HONOR YOU
ALL THE DAYS OF MY LIFE

IN SICKNESS AND IN HEALTH

In this last segment, you get a glimpse of Bill and Mary Gearon's 50 plus years of married life, hear about forgiveness as an essential part of their marriage and have an opportunity to reflect on the marriage vows of commitment and faithfulness. Bill and Mary share some of the strengths that helped them create a deeply loving marriage. These include:

* **God as the third member of their partnership**

* **Going to Church together**

* **Never going to bed angry with each other**

* **Praying through crises and before major decisions**

* **Finding spiritual support as a way of life**

* **Praying daily together**

Think of someone you know who has been married a long time. What do you think are the strengths that have helped them have a lasting marriage?

THE FOUR MOST IMPORTANT WORDS YOU WILL EVER SPEAK TO ONE ANOTHER ARE

"WILL YOU FORGIVE ME?"

Be kind to one another, compassionate, forgiving one another as God has forgiven you in Christ.

Ephesians 4:32

"I promise to love you and honor you all the days of my life..." This vow does not have the words "except when you hurt me" attached. When two people really love each other and live together, hurts and heartache will occur. Fr. Vomund used the analogy of a broken arm. When a bone breaks and **heals properly** that section of bone is stronger than it ever was before the injury. Married couples have a choice - to store each hurt in their hearts and hang on to the pain OR decide to heal the hurt and make the relationship stronger - like the mended arm. **Love IS being willing to ask "Will you forgive me?"** The ability to **give and receive** forgiveness is essential for a successful marriage. Remember, just as good communication is a skill that is learned, so is forgiveness.

Forgiveness is difficult for many people. Here are some reasons people have for withholding forgiveness:

 Check the reasons that relate to your own experiences.

____ The hurt is too deep.

____ If I forgive them, then they will think it's okay to do it again.

____ I want to teach them a lesson so they will know how hurt I am.

____ Forgiving is a sign of weakness.

____ They did the unforgivable.

____ I won't forgive until they say they are sorry.

____ I've already forgiven them for that. They should have learned the first time. I won't forgive a second time.

____ They don't deserve to be forgiven.

____ I will forgive only if they promise never to do it again.

 Do any of the above statements apply to your relationship with your fiancé? If so, give a recent example.

Then Peter approaching asked him, "Lord, if my brother sins against me, how often must I forgive him? As many as seven times?" Jesus answered, "I say to you, not seven times, but seventy-seven times."

Matthew 18:21-22

4. When you have hurt someone (even accidentally), do you:
✔ Check all that apply.

_____ ask the other person to forgive you

_____ say "I'm sorry"

_____ ignore it - do nothing

_____ wait for the other person to bring it up

_____ figure they have hurt you in the past, so now you are even

_____ feel embarrassed and say "I didn't mean it"

_____ try to make it up to the other person

_____ try to get out of the discomfort by saying "I was just kidding"

_____ other_____

WHAT DO YOU SAY?

"I'm Sorry" vs "Will you forgive me?"

When we simply say "I'm sorry," we keep the focus on ourselves. There is no request for a response, no reaching out to the other person. But when we ask "Will you forgive me?" we put the focus on the relationship. We ask for a response, we reach out to the other person. "I'm sorry" may seem like a half-hearted apology. "Will you forgive me?" comes across as a sincere apology AND request to reconcile ... to heal the relationship ... to make it whole again.

So, now what will you say?

5. How do you react when hurt/angry/resentful?
✔ Check all that apply.

_____ ignore it; pretend it did not happen

_____ give the other person the cold shoulder

_____ leave the house/room

_____ use facial expressions to convey my feelings

_____ raise my voice; bang things loudly in the room

_____ share my feelings with the person who hurt me

_____ hold grudges for hours or even days

_____ think about how to get revenge

_____ hold on to the hurt and remember all the other times that person hurt me

_____ other_____

6. Give a recent example of feeling hurt by your fiancé. How did you react? Did you eventually forgive your fiancé?

7. Is your relationship stronger, or will it be, once healing takes place?

 8. Do you hang on to old hurts? Are you ready to bring them up when that, or some other hurt, happens again? Name what you tend to bring up during an argument. When have you said "You always ..." or "You never ..."?

 9. How do you and your fiancé handle the need to forgive each other? Check all that apply.

	Often	Sometimes	Never
We share our feelings openly.	____	____	____
I readily ask for forgiveness.	____	____	____
My fiancé readily asks for forgiveness.	____	____	____
I accept my fiancé's apologies easily.	____	____	____
My fiancé accepts my apologies easily.	____	____	____

> When we don't forgive ourselves, we put ourselves above God. (1)
>
> *Sr. Marlene Halpin*

> Man and woman need the help of the grace that God in his infinite mercy never refuses them. (Cf. Gen 3:21) Without God's help man and woman cannot achieve the union of their lives for which God created them "in the beginning."
>
> *Catechism of the Catholic Church #1608*

Bill and Mary said that from the beginning **God was a third member of their partnership.** God's presence was the key to having their marriage survive. Mary shared that it took a lot of prayer to forgive. Forgiving from the heart is sometimes impossible without God's help. When we hurt so deeply, it is God who provides the grace, strength, courage and compassion to truly forgive. In the Sacrament of Matrimony, we have God's grace to make forgiveness possible. It is God's compassion that lies behind our ability to forgive.

 In what areas do you especially need God's grace to be able to forgive from your heart and to ask for forgiveness? (e.g. holding grudges, wanting revenge, dealing with the hurt, letting go of past hurts...)

HAVE YOU EVER HELD A BEACHBALL UNDER WATER?

Holding a beachball under water takes all of our energy and concentration. It's like holding on to past hurts. It takes all of our energy and concentration and prevents us from free interaction in our relationships. As we add to those hurts, the "ball" gets bigger and more difficult to keep under water. Eventually, the ball of hurts gets too difficult to hold down. The hurts explode into our life. A healthy relationship takes two hands. We cannot hold onto hurts AND build healthy relationships. True forgiveness requires letting go of the hurt to become free to live well and love well again.

SACRAMENT OF RECONCILIATION

The Sacrament of Reconciliation offers Catholics the opportunity to bring our brokenness to God and ask for forgiveness. Through the grace of this Sacrament, we can leave our past behind and go forward with renewed commitment to love as Jesus loves. Engaged couples are encouraged to celebrate the Sacrament of Reconciliation as an added help to deal with past hurts, to better understand weaknesses and to receive forgiveness through God's unconditional love, faithfulness and divine forgiveness. The grace of this sacrament can then empower us to extend this Christ-like love in marriage.

 Have you talked to one another about receiving the Sacrament of Reconciliation before your marriage?

God's plan

The video presented God's plan for marriage as living out the vows of the Sacrament. God's plan is simply to "love one another in good times and bad, for better for worse, for richer for poorer, in sickness and health, 'till death do us part." We saw Mary loving Bill by putting drops in his eyes for his glaucoma. Her love and caring for him were apparent in her gentleness and compassion. Taking time to lovingly do the little things is what loving each other is all about.

 Name a "little thing" that your fiancé does for you.

Father Eugene Morris said...

"The Church asks a great deal of you as a married couple: a faithful, loving, life-giving, enduring relationship. In return, you may expect from the Church that She, through her teachings, her priests, and her people, will support and sustain you both."

Bill said that "they" stayed faithful and God stayed faithful. Their commitment to their marriage helped them through the darkest part of their journey. "Marriage is hard work. If you are willing to sacrifice, then you can get through the hard times. There's a gift waiting for you at the end - the gift of your relationship." Bill and Mary experienced the natural cycles of **romance, disillusionment and joy** in their marriage. They found that by letting God grace the sacrificial times, they found joy.

 Describe what you want your relationship to look like in 40 or 50 years. What do you want people to say about your marriage?

Bill said...

"If you are really stuck, ask yourselves 'What can we do to help the marriage to win?' We might both lose a little of what we want, but we will get something better."

IT'S IN THE LITTLE THINGS THAT WE BEGIN TO SEE AND UNDERSTAND WHAT IT MEANS TO **BE** THE

SACRAMENT OF MATRIMONY-

THE ONLY ENFLESHED SIGN TO THE WORLD OF HOW MUCH GOD LOVES ALL OF US.

 After reflecting on the meaning of the Sacrament of Matrimony ask yourself: Do I want to be married in the Catholic community and to become a sacramental couple? Am I willing to accept this vocation?

A Couple's Prayer

Dear Good and Gracious God,
Thank you for helping us to find one another and
for our desire to spend the rest of our lives loving each other.

Help us to respond to your call to love truly
with the love of Jesus.

Help us to create a marriage that includes
You as a full partner.

Turn our weaknesses into strengths
and heal our brokenness.

Help us to do what is good;

For we are yours, empowered with your grace
Let our love shine
and make a difference in the world.

Amen.

The four most important words you will ever speak to one another are **"Will you forgive me?"**

I PROMISE TO LOVE YOU AND HONOR YOU

ALL THE DAYS OF MY LIFE

Works Cited

Chapter 2

(1) Smalley, Gary. *Hidden Keys to Loving Relationships*. VHS, The Gary Smalley Seminar. Relationships Today, Inc., 1988.

(2) Center for Marriage and Family. *Time, Sex, and Money: The First Five Years of Marriage*. Omaha, NE: Creighton University, 2000.

(3) Center for Marriage & Family. *Ministry to Interchurch Marriages*. Omaha, NE: Creighton University, 1999.

Chapter 3

(1) National Council on Alcoholism and Drug Abuse
8790 Manchester Rd. St. Louis, MO 63144
www.ncada-stl.org
314.962.3456

(2) Problem Gambling
www.addictions.net

(3) National Eating Disorder Association
www.nationaleatingdisorders.org
Information and Referral Helpline: 1.800.931.2237

(4) Domestic Violence
www.domesticviolence.com

(5) Sexaholics Anonymous
P.O. Box 111910 Nashville, TN 37222
615.331.6230
www.saico@sa.org

(6) Wright, Norman. *So You're Getting Married: The Keys to Building a Strong, Lasting Marriage*. Richardson, TX: Grace Products Corporation, 1995.

(7) Buonarroti, Michelangelo. (1475- 1564).

Chapter 4

(1) Pope John Paul II. *Familiaris Consortio*. 1981.
http://www.vatican.va/holy_father/john_paul_ii/apost_exhortations/documents/hf_jp-ii_exh_19811122_familiaris-consortio_en.html

(2) Center for Marriage and Family. *Time, Sex, and Money: The First Five Years of Marriage*. Omaha, NE: Creighton University, 2000.

(3) Foch FSC, Carl and Pharr, Virginia. *Creating a Christian Lifestyle*. Winona, MN: St. Mary's Press,1996.

(4) Centers for Disease Control
www.cdc.gov

(5) Pope Paul VI. *Gaudium et Spes*. Documents of Vatican II, 1965.

(6) Domestic Violence
www.ncvc.org/infolinks.INFO14.htm

(7) Domestic Abuse
www.silcom.com

(8)   Maloof, David. "Why I'll Never Move In' Again." Redbook, Jan. 1994. p. 108-109.

(9)   Scott, K.C. " Mom, I Want to Live with My Boyfriend." Reader's Digest, Feb 1994. p. 77-80.

(10) Healy, James, PhD. *Living Together and Christian Commitment.* Rooted in Love. Allen, TX: Tabor Publishing, 1999.

(11) Sr. Barbara Markey. "Preparing Cohabiting Couples for Marriage." (VHS and Study Guide) Omaha, NE: FOCCUS, Inc.,1999.

(12) Center for Marriage and Family. *Time, Sex, and Money: The First Five Years of Marriage.* Omaha, NE: Creighton University, 2000.

Chapter 5

(1)   Hannibal, Susan. "DTR with God."

(2)   Covey, Stephen R. *The 7 Habits of Highly Effective People.* New York: Simon & Shuster, 1990.

(3)   Midgley, John and Midgley, Susan. *A Decision to Love.* 1992. Mystic, CT: Twenty-Third Publications,1992.

(4)   Gordon, Lori. *Passage to Intimacy.* Weston, FL: PAIRS Foundation, LTD., 1993.

Chapter 6

(1)   Center for Marriage and Family. *Time, Sex, and Money: The First Five Years of Marriage.* Omaha, NE: Creighton University, 2000.

(2)   Consumer Credit Counseling Services. "The Newlyweds' Guide to Money Management." 1998.

(3)   Center for Marriage and Family. *Time, Sex, and Money: The First Five Years of Marriage.* Omaha, NE: Creighton University, 2000.

Chapter 7

(1)   Pope Paul VI. *Gaudium et Spes.* Documents of Vatican II, 1965.

(2)   Pope Paul VI. *Humanae Vitae.* Boston, MA: Daughters of St. Paul, 1968.

(3)   Department of Natural Family Planning. "What Can Natural Family Planning Do For You." Archdiocese of Saint Louis, MO.

(4)   Hilgers,Thomas. *An Introduction Booklet for New Users.* Omaha, NE: Pope Paul VI Institute Press, 2001.

(5)   Pope Paul VI. *Humanae Vitae.* Boston, MA: Daughters of St. Paul, 1968.

(6)   Gertzoff, Ann and McClenahan, Carolyn. *Step-kids: A Survival Guide for Teenagers in Stepfamilies.* New York: Walker and Company, 1984. pg. 161.

Chapter 8

(1)   Halpin, Marlene. *Forgiving: Present Perfect.* Dubuque, Iowa: Wm. C. Brown, 1987.

Bibliography

Buonarroti, Michelangelo. (1475- 1564).

Coyle-Hennessey, Bobbi. *A Guide to Marrying Again: Once More With Love*. Notre Dame, IN: Ave Maria Press, 1993.

Centers for Disease Control, www.cdc.gov.

Center for Marriage and Family. *Marriage Preparation in the Catholic Church: Getting It Right, Report of a Study on the Value of Marriage Preparation in the Catholic Church for Couples Married One through Eight Years*. Omaha, NE: Creighton University, 1995.

Center for Marriage & Family. *Ministry to Interchurch Marriages*. Omaha, NE: Creighton University, 1999.

Center for Marriage and Family. *Time, Sex, and Money: The First Five Years of Marriage*. Omaha, NE: Creighton University, 2000.

Covey, Stephen R. *The 7 Habits of Highly Effective People*. New York: Simon & Shuster, 1990.

Domestic Abuse, www.silcom.com.

Domestic Violence, www.domesticviolence.com.

Foch FSC, Carl and Pharr, Virginia. *Creating a Christian Lifestyle*. Winona, MN: St. Mary's Press,1996.

Gertzoff, Ann and McClenahan, Carolyn. *Step-kids: A Survival Guide for Teenagers in Stepfamilies*. New York: Walker and Company, 1984.

Gordon, Lori. *Passage to Intimacy*. Weston, FL: PAIRS Foundation, LTD., 1993.

Halpin, Marlene. *Forgiving: Present Perfect*. Dubuque, Iowa: Wm. C. Brown, 1987.

Healy, James, PhD. *Living Together and Christian Commitment*. Rooted in Love. Allen, TX: Tabor Publishing, 1999.

Hilgers,Thomas. *An Introduction Booklet for New Users*. Omaha, NE: Pope Paul VI Institute Press, 2001.
Kilcourse, George. *Double Belonging*. New York/Mahwah, NJ: Paulist Press, 1992.

Maloof, David. "Why I'll Never Move In' Again." Redbook, Jan. 1994.

Markey, Sr. Barbara. "Preparing Cohabiting Couples for Marriage." (VHS and Study Guide)
Omaha, NE: FOCCUS, Inc.,1999.

Midgley, John and Midgley, Susan. *A Decision to Love*. 1992. Mystic, CT: Twenty-Third Publications,1992.

National Council on Alcoholism and Drug Abuse, 8790 Manchester Rd. St. Louis, MO 63144
www.ncada-stl.org, 314·962·3456

National Eating Disorder Association, www.nationaleatingdisorders.org.
Information and Referral Helpline: 1-800-931-2237

The National Marriage Project. *The State of Our Unions 2001: The Social Health of Marriage in America*. Piscataway, NJ: Rutgers, The State University of New Jersey, 2001.

Pope John Paul II. *Familiaris Consortio*. 1981.
http://www.vatican.va/holy_father/john_paul_ii/apost_exhortations/documents/hf_jp-ii_exh_19811122_familiaris-consortio_en.html

Pope Paul VI. *Gaudium et Spes*. Documents of Vatican II, 1965.

Pope Paul VI. *Humanae Vitae*. Boston, MA: Daughters of St. Paul, 1968.

Problem Gambling, www.addictions.net.

Sexaholics Anonymous, P.O. Box 111910 Nashville, TN 37222, 615·331·6230, www.saico@sa.org.

Scott, K.C. "Mom, I Want to Live with My Boyfriend." Reader's Digest, Feb 1994.

Smalley, Gary. *Hidden Keys to Loving Relationships*. VHS, The Gary Smalley Seminar. Relationships Today, Inc., 1988.

Wright, Norman. *So You're Getting Married: The Keys to Building a Strong, Lasting Marriage*.Richardson, TX: Grace Products Corporation, 1995.

Resources

Books

1. *Prayers for Married Couples*
   Bartkowski, Renee
   Liguori Press
   ISBN 0-89243-301-9

2. *Please Understand Me: Character & Temperament Types*
   Bates, Marilyn and David Keirsey
   Prometheus Book Company
   ISBN 0-9606954-0-0

3. *The Five Love Languages: How to Express Heartfelt Commitment to Your Mate*
   Chapman, Gary
   Northfield Publishing, ISBN 1-881273-15-6

4. *Prayer Book for Engaged Couples*
   Fleming, Austin
   Liturgy Training Publications
   ISBN 0-929650-23-9

5. *Passage to Intimacy*
   Gordon, Lori H., Ph.D.
   ISBN 0-671-79596-1

6. *Para el Nuevo milenio: Un recurso para las parejas que se esta'n preparando para el matrimonio cristiano: En Las Buenas y Para Siempre*
   Ruhnke, Robert, C.SS.R, D.Min.
   ISBN: 0-9677223-2-2

7. *A Resource for Couples Preparing for Christian Marriage For Better and For Ever.*
   Ruhnke, Robert, C.SS.R, D.Min.
   Litho Press, Inc.
   ISBN: 0-9677223-0-6

8. *Beginning Your Marriage*
   Thomas, John L., S.J.
   ACTA Publications
   ISBN 0-915388-24-3

Audio Cassette

9. *Rooted in Love,* Dr. James Healy

Addictions and Compulsions Resources

10. Al-Anon Family Group Headquarters
    1.800.344.2666

11. Center for the Prevention of Sexual and Domestic Violence
    www.cpsdv.org

12. Center for Substance Abuse Treatment
    1.800.729.6686 or 1.800.662.HELP
    Internet: www.samhsa.gov

13. National Eating Disorder Association,
    www.nationaleatingdisorders.org
    Information and Referral Helpline: 1.800.931.2237

14. National Council on Problem Gambling, Inc.
    www.ncpgambling.org
    1.800.522.4700

15. Sexaholics Anonymous
    P.O. Box 111910
    Nashville, TN 37222
    615.331.6901
    www.saico@sa.org

16. "When I Call for Help"
    Domestic Violence
    available in English and Spanish
    US Bishop Letter
    www.nccbuscc.org/laity/help.htm

Sexuality and Planning Your Family

17. *Postfertilization Effects of Oral Contraceptives and Their Relationship to Informed Consent*
    Larimore, Walter and Joseph Stanford
    Archives of Family Medication

18. *Good News about Sex and Marriage: Answers to Your Honest Questions about Catholic Teaching*
    West, Christopher
    Servant Publications
    ISBN 1-56955-214-2

19. Billings Ovulation Method
    http://boma-usa.org

20. Creighton Model Fertility Care
    http://creightonmodel.com

21. Creighton Model Fertility Care System
    An Introduction Booklet for New Users
    Thomas W.Hilgers, MD
    Pope Paul VI Institute
    Thomas W. Hegas MD
    6901 Mercy Rd.
    Omaha, NE 68106
    www.popepaulvi.com

22. Symto Thermal Method
    (Couple to Couple League)
    www.ccli.org

DTR Communication Skills

23. The PAIRS Foundation
    (Practical Application of Intimate Relationship Skills)
    1.888.485.7080
    www.PAIRS.com

CONSUMER DEBT COUNSELING ®

and Consumer Credit Counseling Service-St. Louis

The Newlyweds' Guide To Money Management

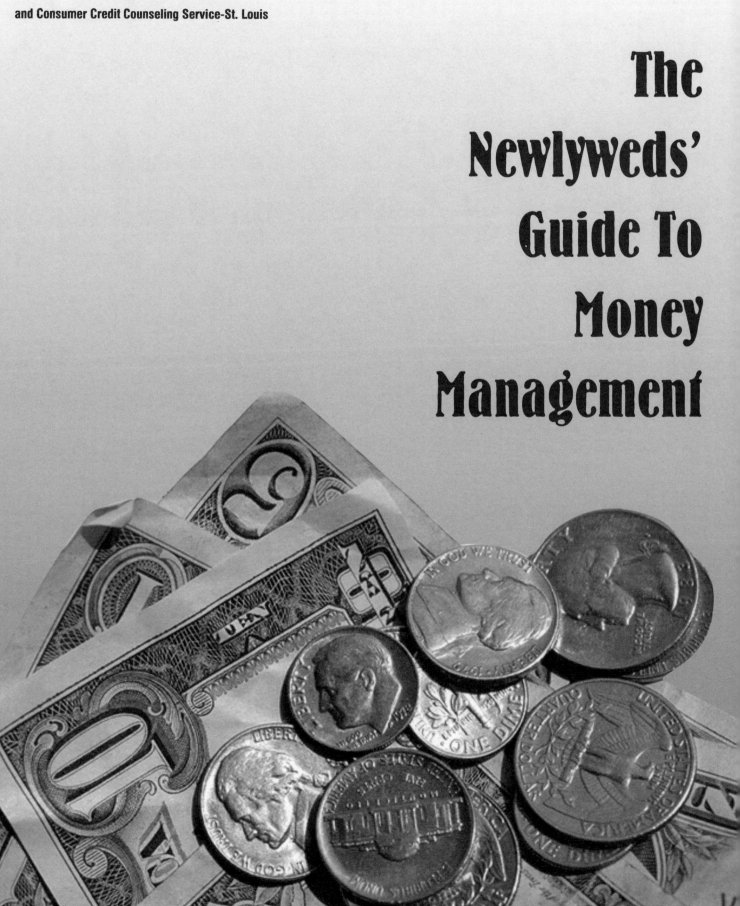

Table Of Contents

Follow The Three Basic Steps

One of the greatest satisfactions in life is having a sense of control over your finances. Through careful planning and use of money management techniques that anyone can learn, a family can feel more confident about its ability to live within its means, reduce debt, handle emergencies and save for the future.

Understanding how to manage money--and developing the discipline to do it well--can make a real difference in your life. The tips, guidelines, worksheets and quizzes that follow will help you determine what will work best for you. They are organized to help you take the three basic steps to successful money management:

- Assessing your current financial situation
- Setting financial goals
- Developing a budget

It does take some effort to follow all three steps completely. However, you will find detailed instructions and basic worksheets in this guide to help you every step of the way.

Tip: You may wish to copy the blank worksheets in this book before you begin to fill them out so that you will have a ready-made fresh supply every time you update your money management records and plan.

Rate Yourself!

Most of us are creatures of habit when it comes to handling (or mishandling) our finances. To start your self-assessment--and motivate yourself to do better--take this brief quiz.

As a rule, do you:	ALWAYS	SOMETIMES	NEVER
1. Pay the rent/mortgage payment and utility bills on time?			
2. Save 10 percent of your net income?			
3. Try to keep three months of your net income in reserve for emergencies?			
4. Plan ahead for large expenses such as taxes and insurance?			
5. Set goals and keep a budget for your net income?			
6. Spend no more than 20 percent of your net income for credit payments, excluding home mortgage?			
7. Comparison shop for the purchase of most items?			
8. Use credit only for expensive purchases or when you have the money in the bank to cover the charge?			
9. Balance your checkbook every month?			
10. Keep yourself financially updated by reading consumer articles?			
TOTALS:			

SCORING:
Give yourself 0 points for each NEVER answer; 1 point for each SOMETIMES; and 2 points for every ALWAYS. Compute your total score and see how you rate.

Zero-ten: Time to take better control of your money by adopting more effective money management skills.

Eleven-fifteen: Reflects a good effort, but you can better your score--and your finances--with a few changes.

Sixteen-twenty: The road to success! Continue to make money management a priority in your household.

Determine Your Monthly Income

To realistically assess your financial situation, you need to develop a **complete** picture of your income. Your evaluation must take into account all regular and periodic income in your family (*gross income);* all paycheck or salary deductions such as taxes, insurance, savings, pension, FICA and union dues; and the amount that remains after deductions (*net income)*.

Worksheet instructions:

A. Monthly Gross Income section

List **all sources of regular earned monthly income** of all individuals living in the household involved in the family budget. This should include full, part-time and self-employment income. List the amount of income received before deductions. (If you are paid weekly, multiply your weekly gross pay by 4.3 to get your monthly gross income. If you receive a paycheck every other week, multiply by 2.2.) Indicate tips, bonuses and overtime as well.

In addition, list **monthly income from other sources**. Remember this is income that can be counted on a regular basis even though it may not be from employment. Examples would include AFDC, maintenance, Social Security, child support, disability, etc.

Finally, don't forget to include **sporadic income** such as bonus checks, income tax refunds, etc. (divided into monthly portions) under "other" income category.

Add up columns in this section to determine *total monthly gross income.*

A. Gross Income	Income #1	Income #2	Income #3	Total
Wages/Salary	$1,000.00	$800.00		$1,800.00
Part-Time Work			$75.00	$75.00
Total Monthly Gross Income	$1,000.00	$800.00	$75.00	$1,875.00

B. Monthly Deductions section

List **all monthly deductions from each source of income**. (Loans owed to a credit union are excluded from this list and will be calculated later as part of your Debt Reduction Plan.)

Add up columns in this section to determine *total monthly deductions.*

B. Deductions	Income #1	Income #2	Income #3	Total
Federal Taxes	$100.00	$80.00	$7.50	$187.50
State Taxes	$10.00	$8.00	$ .75	$18.75
Total Monthly Deductions	$110.00	$88.00	$8.25	$206.25

C. Monthly Net Income section

Enter your **total gross income from section A of the worksheet** and your total deductions from section B. To determine your *monthly net income*, subtract deductions from gross income.

C. Monthly Net Income	Income #1	Income #2	Income #3	Total
Total Monthly Gross Income	$1,000.00	$800.00	$75.00	$1,875.00
Minus Total Monthly Deductions	$110.00	$88.00	$8.25	$206.25
Equals Monthly Net Income	$890.00	$712.00	$66.75	$1,668.75

Determine Your Monthly Income

Monthly Income Worksheet

A. Gross Income	Income #1	Income #2	Income #3	Total
Wages/Salary				
Part-Time Work				
Self-Employment				
Bonus/Overtime/Tips				
Child Support				
Maintenance				
Rental Property				
AFDC				
Disability Compensation				
Unemployment Insurance				
Food Stamps				
Pension				
Social Security				
Interest/Dividends				
National Guard/Reserves				
Other				
Total Monthly Gross Income				

B. Deductions	Income #1	Income #2	Income #3	Total
Federal Taxes				
State Taxes				
Local Taxes				
Social Security (FICA)/Medicare				
Child Support				
Medical Insurance				
Union Dues				
Savings				
Pension Plan				
Other				
Total Monthly Deductions				

C. Monthly Net Income	Income #1	Income #2	Income #3	Total
Total Monthly Gross Income				
Minus Total Monthly Deductions				
Equals Monthly Net Income				

Determine Your Monthly Expenses

Once you have determined your monthly net income, you are ready to tackle your family's expenses. To be most useful in your planning efforts, your figures must be both comprehensive and accurate. You cannot overlook even the smallest expenditures if you want to have a true picture of where your money really goes every month. On the other hand, don't give up if you can't remember where every cent went in recent months. Do your best to reconstruct the past and set the stage immediately for better record-keeping for the future.

Tip: Accurate records mean just that. Make sure each member of your family understands that every expenditure--from a 50-cent candy bar at school to a $1 lottery ticket at the gas station--should be written down.

Records Are The Key

To track expenses, most families will need the following record-keeping systems:

- A checkbook register to record every check and/or debit card purchase
- Tracking forms for recording out-of-pocket expenditures for each family member
- A credit card purchase tracking form
- And, a well-organized filing system to make all of your record-keeping easier.

Maintaining And Balancing Your Checkbook

While checks and checkbooks may come in all colors and designs, they all offer the opportunity to carefully record the details of your financial activity. To maximize your checkbook's useful features, utilize your checkbook register to record every transaction you make, i.e. standard deposits or withdrawals. Don't forget to note ATM transactions, any service charges on your account and transfers from other accounts.

Tip: Debit card purchases that electronically draw on money in your checking account need to be recorded immediately. Be sure to write down each transaction in your checkbook in the same detailed manner as you would list a check.

Here are some basic steps to help you keep an error-free register and to know exactly whether or not you have enough money in your bank account to cover the checks you write:
- For each check, enter in the appropriate spaces the check number, the date, to whom you wrote the check and why, and the amount of the check. It's important to subtract the amount from your current balance right away so that you don't overestimate how much money you have in your account.
- For each deposit, enter in the appropriate spaces the date, the source of the money and the deposit amount. Immediately add this sum to your current balance.
- Make entries for ATM transactions, transfers and service charges in the same way, adding or subtracting when appropriate.

Once a month, you will receive a statement from your bank listing every transaction made on that account. To balance your account, compare your checkbook register to your bank statement.

Here's how to balance your account:
- Using your check number as a reference point, put your canceled checks in numerical order.
- Make sure your canceled checks match what you've listed in your register.
- Put a check mark on each canceled check and the corresponding amount in your register.
- Be sure you have subtracted all service fees and have added all interest charges shown on your statement.
- Subtract automatic payments and add automatic deposits shown on your statement, which you haven't recorded already.
- On the back of the statement, list all outstanding checks and their amounts.
- Total the amount of the outstanding checks.
- Subtract the total of outstanding checks from the "new balance" listed on the bank statement.
- Add in any deposits you have made that do not appear on the statement.
- Your checkbook balance should agree with the bank balance.
- If these figures don't agree, check your arithmetic and your entries again.
- Notify the bank if the error appears to be theirs. If necessary, ask bank personnel to help you balance correctly.

Tip: Reconciling your checkbook each and every month makes the task simpler and helps you avoid costly errors that could result in bounced checks and credit problems.
Tracking Out-of- Pocket Cash Spending

Tracking Out-Of-Pocket Cash Spending

A good way to begin evaluating your family's out-of-pocket cash spending is to have each person track his or her purchases for three months. Everyone should carry a personal form, piece of notebook paper or small notebook to record all out-of-pocket spending--from gum to video rentals--as it occurs. The record should include the date, amount spent, what was purchased and category, such as entertainment, food or clothing.

Tip: You will probably be surprised by how much you really do spend out-of-pocket--and by how simple it would be to decrease the constant cash drain on your wallet.

OUT-OF-POCKET CASH SPENDING TRACKING FORM

Fill in your own categories.   Dates _August 1_ to _August 28_

$ Food In	$ Food Out	$ Gas	$ Recreation	$ Clothes	$ Misc.	$ Parking
Groceries	Movie Snack	$10.00	Movie	Nylons	Envelopes	$5.50/wk.
		13.00	$9.00	$3.00	Potholder	
$89.46	$8.00	10.00			Towel	$22.00
67.83	17.00	10.00	$9.00	$3.00		
93.61	$25.00	9.00			$7.38	
73.26		$52.00				
2.70						
$326.86						

OUT-OF-POCKET CASH SPENDING TRACKING FORM

Fill in your own categories.   Dates_____to_____

$	$	$	$	$	$	$

Tracking Credit Card Purchases

When tracking spending, be certain to include credit card spending as well. Develop your own system or use the form below.

Maintain a monthly file of your credit card receipts. Verify their posting on your monthly credit card statements. When using credit as part of your monthly spending plan, try to always have a repayment plan in mind that fits in with your overall financial goals.

CREDIT CARD PURCHASES TRACKING FORM

Card:

Date	Purchase	Amount
Total:		

Card:

Date	Purchase	Amount
Total:		

Card:

Date	Purchase	Amount
Total:		

Card:

Date	Purchase	Amount
Total:		

Organizing A Filing System

An essential part of taking control of your finances is keeping records. Get yourself organized to make your task easier.

You will need:
1. A looseleaf notebook and filler paper
2. Dividers for notebooks (optional)
3. A cardboard filing box or any box that will hold file folders
4. A box of file folders
5. A box or pleated folder for credit card receipts

The notebook should include:

1. Financial goals list
2. Personal directory-a list of family and friends who should be notified in the event of your death or catastrophe
3. Professional directory-include every professional involved in your affairs: physician, clergy, lawyer, banker, etc.
4. List of credit card numbers
5. List of bank and brokerage accounts
6. Location of documents, i.e. safe deposit box
7. Monthly spending plans
8. List of wallet contents
9. Net worth statement (list of assets, debts)

The file box should include all current material. There should be separate files for:

1. The house or apartment where you live
2. Each bank account
3. Each insurance company
4. Each vehicle
5. Each utility company
6. Warranties and product instruction books
7. Employee benefits packages/information
8. Health records
9. Each credit card, bank loan, etc.
10. Each pet or one pet file
11. Magazine and CD club subscriptions

As your finances become more complex, rent a safe deposit box to keep these personal and financial documents:

1. Birth, baptism and marriage certificates
2. Social security cards
3. Passports
4. Insurance policies
5. Will and living wills
6. Power of attorney
7. Divorce decree
8. Military discharge papers
9. Naturalization papers
10. Diploma, awards
11. Land abstracts, deeds, title policies
12. Appraisals of personal property
13. Bills of sale
14. Bonds, certificates of deposit
15. Individual retirement accounts
16. Legal agreements
17. Personal property pictures/inventory
18. Securities, stock certificates
19. Property tax receipts
20. Family death certificates

Tip: Items used for income tax purposes should be saved for seven years. Your paycheck stubs can be thrown out after you receive your W-2 forms and check the numbers. You may want to keep utility bill stubs for a year for comparison or house sale purposes. Keep records of purchases until the account has been paid and the last check clears the bank.

Classifying Your Monthly Expenses

To get a better sense of your monthly expenses and to identify ones that can be reduced most easily, list your expenses under the appropriate classification: fixed, variable or periodic.

Fixed expenses, such as car or child support payments, stay the same from month to month and are often the most difficult type to reduce. For example, a mortgage payment is a fixed expense that can only be changed by selling the home and moving or refinancing the mortgage. This is not to say that fixed expenses cannot be changed. Rather, it may take a longer time to reduce fixed expenses than it would to lower variable or periodic ones.

Variable expenses are expenditures such as gasoline, parking and dry cleaning that vary from week to week or month to month. They are easier to change; therefore, if you want to spend less, pay close attention to variable expenses. For example, food is a variable expense that can be reduced by eating out less often or by instituting a change in diet that would provide the same nutrition for the family at a lower cost.

Periodic expenses, which may often be forgotten until they come due, are frequently the culprit in wrecking a family's budget plan. Periodic expenses are those that generally occur only once or twice a year. They include such items as gifts, car repair and insurance, medications, eyeglasses, clothing and home maintenance.

Estimate Your Expenses

Fill in your estimates of monthly expenses in each category on the Monthly Expenses worksheet on the next two pages. You may not have expenditures for all entries and may need to add entries that are specific to your family.

The simplest type of expenses to estimate are, of course, the *fixed* ones, which should be the same amount of money every month. Indicate your estimated monthly fixed expenses on the worksheet. *Variable expenses* can be more difficult to estimate precisely. Don't let that put you off from trying, however. The best way to develop a realistic estimate of your variable expenses is to review your previous expenses in this category and look for patterns of spending over several months. Then come up with a reasonable monthly average for each section and list it on the worksheet. *Periodic expenses* are easiest to plan for if you determine a monthly average payment based on your estimated annual total for each anticipated expenditure. In other words, first estimate your total periodic expenses for the coming year in each worksheet category, such as car repair and medications. Then, divide each expense estimate by 12 and record it on the worksheet separately as an estimated monthly periodic expense.

Tip: Use your completed worksheet estimates to seek out expenses that can be adjusted or reduced. Try ideas such as eliminating cable television, forming a baby-sitting co-op, reducing the number of monthly long- distance telephone calls or eliminating other telephone convenience services such as call waiting, caller ID, etc.

Record And Evaluate Actual Expenses

In the center column, record the actual expenditure (what was actually spent) for the month in each category. Note possible cutbacks in the Potential Reductions column. Continue to work with the Monthly Expenses worksheet to find ways to spend less in the variable and periodic categories, especially if debt reduction is your goal. Begin to view your spending in terms of "needs" versus "wants." Obviously, a need is more important than a want. Remember, record keeping is extremely important during the beginning of a budget as you are trying to find a plan that works for you.

Monthly Expenses Worksheet

FIXED EXPENSES (Amounts Stay The Same Month To Month)	Estimated Monthly Expenses	Actual Expenditures	Potential Reductions
Rent/Mortgage			
Second Mortgage/Home Equity Loan			
Lot Rent/Subdivision/Condo Fee			
Homeowner's/Renter's Insurance			
Real Estate/Personal Property Tax			
Car Payment/Lease			
Second Car Payment/Lease			
Emergency Fund/Savings			
Student Loans			
Child Support/Maintenance			
Day Care			
Medical Insurance			
Life Insurance			
Cable Television			
Checking Account Fees			
Professional or Service Org. Dues			
Home Security Systems			
Other			
TOTAL FIXED EXPENSES			
VARIABLE EXPENSES (Paid Monthly, But Amount Paid Can Vary, Use Averages)			
Electric			
Gas/Propane/Wood			
Telephone/Long Distance/Internet			
Cellular Phone/Pager			
Garbage			
Water/Sewer			
Groceries (Food Only)			
Food at Work			
School Lunches			
Dining Out			
Household/Misc./Paper, Cleaning Prod.			
Personal Hygiene Items			
Tobacco/Alcohol			

Monthly Expenses Worksheet (cont.)

VARIABLE EXPENSES	Estimated Monthly Expenses	Actual Expenditures	Potential Reductions
Gasoline			
Bus, Car Pool, Parking			
Laundromat/Dry Cleaning			
Barber/Beauty Shop			
Newspaper/Magazine			
Tuition/Books/Supplies			
Children's Allowance/Spending Money			
Recreation			
Lessons (Dance, Music, etc.)/Sports Fees			
Pet Expenses (Food, Vet Fees)			
Church/Charity			
Postage			
Other			
TOTAL VARIABLE EXPENSES			
PERIODIC EXPENSES (Do Not Occur Every Month: Divide Annual Cost By 12)			
Car Repair/Maintenance			
Car Insurance			
Auto License/Inspection			
Doctor/Dentist			
Medications/Prescriptions			
Eyeglasses/Contact Lenses			
Clothing/Shoes			
Home Repair/Maintenance			
Appliance Repair/Maintenance			
Gifts (Birthdays, Holidays, etc.)			
Other			
TOTAL PERIODIC EXPENSES			

TOTAL MONTHLY NET INCOME (Listed in Green Box on Page 4)	**+**	
MINUS TOTAL MONTHLY EXPENSES (Fixed + Variable + Periodic)	**−**	
EQUALS TOTAL EXCESS AVAILABLE FOR DEBT REDUCTION	**=**	
MINUS TOTAL MONTHLY PAYMENT TO CREDITORS (Listed in Green Box on Page 19)	**−**	
EQUALS TOTAL EXCESS (OR DEFICIT)	**=**	

Monthly Expenses Worksheet

A Family Affair

Developing specific financial goals--and putting them in writing--is a great motivator for gaining control of your money. Keep in mind that your goals may need to be adjusted every six to eight months in response to changes in your family's income, needs and priorities.

Make goal-setting a family affair. Children benefit from sharing ideas and needs while learning more about handling money. In general, create goals that are precise, practical and positive. Then pull together to achieve them.

Write Out Your Goals Worksheet

Use this worksheet or your own system to list your goals. Then, do what you must to reach them.

SHORT-RANGE GOALS (Within 12 Months)

Goal	Date Needed	Cost Estimate	Amount Already Saved	Amount Needed Per Month To Reach Goal

MID-RANGE GOALS (Within 1 To 3 Years)

Goal	Date Needed	Cost Estimate	Amount Already Saved	Amount Needed Per Month To Reach Goal

LONG-RANGE GOALS (Within 3 To 5 Years)

Goal	Date Needed	Cost Estimate	Amount Already Saved	Amount Needed Per Month To Reach Goal

Budgeting Works

Successful money management begins with creating a household budget. Although the process may seem difficult and time-consuming, it is vital to gaining control of your finances as well as reaching your financial goals.

A working budget is more than a blueprint for the spending of future income. It becomes the family's plan for saving as well as for spending and a road map for reaching your goals. While it requires you to estimate your available income and to make decisions about spending those funds, your budget will help you implement a money management plan for your future.

A successful budget should be judged by whether it helps your family:

- Increase savings
- Repay debt
- Prevent impulse spending
- Decide what you can afford
- Identify expenses that can be reduced

There is no single "budget formula" that is successful for all households. Every household chooses to spend its money in its own way, to meet its own needs. The secret to successful budgeting is to develop a realistic plan that is workable for your family and unique circumstances, and then follow it.

Tip: Once you have written out your monthly income, monthly expenses and financial goals with the worksheets provided, you have all the tools you need to determine your budget. You know where you are financially and where you want to be. Now, begin to formulate a budget that will tell you how to get there through better debt management and increased savings.

Managing Debt

For many people, the most difficult part of preparing a workable budget to meet their goals is debt management. Loans and credit cards can be helpful financial tools. However, when credit gets out of control, it can be costly and even disastrous to a family's financial health.

As a first step in developing your budget, it's essential that you evaluate your current use of credit, set goals for using it successfully and investigate ways of reducing it if necessary.

15

Do You Have Your Credit Use Under Control?

To assess your current skill at managing debt and credit use, take the following quiz. For married couples, both spouses should answer the questions.

	YES	NO
1. Are you borrowing money or using credit cards to pay for items that you formerly purchased with cash?	___	___
2. Is more than 20 percent of your net income going to pay debts (excluding home mortgage payment)?	___	___
3. Are you paying bills with money intended for something else?	___	___
4. Are you dipping into your savings to pay current bills?	___	___
5. If you or your spouse lost your job, do you have less than three months take-home pay in a savings account?	___	___
6. Can you usually only make the minimum payment on your credit cards?	___	___
7. Are you extending repayment schedules–paying in 60 or 90 days bills that you once paid in 30 days?	___	___
8. Are you near, at, or over the limit on your credit cards?	___	___
9. Do you take out a new loan before the old one is paid off or take out a new one to pay off an existing loan?	___	___
10. Are you unsure of how much you owe (within $50)?	___	___
11. Do you habitually pay your bills late?	___	___
12. Do you charge more each month than you make in payments?	___	___
13. Do you use a cash advance on one credit card to make payments on other credit cards?	___	___
14. Has a collection agency called recently about an overdue bill?	___	___
15. Are you threatened with repossession of your car, cancellation of your credit cards or other legal actions?	___	___

SCORING:

If you answered "no" to all questions, you know how to manage credit well.

If you answered "yes" to any of the questions 1 through 5, you should cut back on credit use and be alert for other signs of overspending.

A "yes" to any of the questions 6 through 10 could mean you are heading for financial trouble. Consider getting help in drawing up a realistic budget. Put away your credit cards and eliminate all unnecessary spending until your spending is under control.

If you answered "yes" to any of the questions 11 through 15, you are in serious trouble and should seek credit counseling immediately.

Debt-Management Goal:
Follow The "Twenty Percent" Rule

How do you determine what level of debt is reasonable to carry at your income level? A good rule of thumb to follow is this:

Never spend more than 20 percent of your net income on the total of these monthly payments:

- Auto loan
- Credit card monthly payments
- Installment loan monthly payments
- Personal loan monthly payments

If you include your monthly rent or mortgage, never exceed 40 percent of your take-home pay for the total of these monthly expenditures.

17

Developing Your Debt Reduction Plan

If you have determined that your debt load is preventing you from reaching your long-term goals, start now to reduce your debt.

The first step is to determine exactly how much you currently owe. Using recent billing statements, payment books, loan agreements and other documents, list all of your outstanding debt on the Debt Reduction Plan worksheet on page 19. Be sure to include all retail balances, charge card balances, credit union loans (even those that are deducted from your paycheck), personal loans, medical/dental bills, legal bills, etc. It is important to include all unpaid balances, even if you have stopped making payments on them.

As you list them, arrange your accounts in order, from the highest to the lowest annual percentage rate (APR) charged. Using your most recent statements, list the outstanding balances and the minimum payments due each month. Include the due dates to help in planning your repayment schedule. Total the minimum payments. If you are able to commit extra income to accelerate your debt repayment (even if it is only a small amount), add this to the total minimum payments. This becomes your monthly debt repayment amount.

When one account is paid off, use that money to increase the payment on the account at the top of the list. This then becomes the new payment amount for the account with the highest APR. Make at least the minimum payment each due date on each outstanding account. Continue this process until all debts are paid in full. Note: This process assumes that you are not adding any additional debt.

EXAMPLE:

	APR	Balance	Min. Payment
Brady's Department Store	23%	$2,000	$45.00+15.00*
Credit Card	18%	2,500	41.00
Tom's Hardware	18%	300	20.00
Dr. Smith	0	750	10.00

Total Minimum Payment: $116.00
Extra to be paid each month: 15.00*
Monthly debt reduction amount to be included in budget: $131.00

Monthly payments to creditors under debt reduction plan:

Brady's Department Store	$45.00+15.00=$60.00
Credit Card	41.00
Tom's Hardware	20.00
Dr. Smith	10.00
Total Monthly Payment to Creditors:	$131.00

Debt Reduction Plan Worksheet

TOTAL MONTHLY PAYMENT TO CREDITORS

Creditor	Account #	APR	Current Balance	Minimum Payment	Due Date	Notes

TOTAL MONTHLY PAYMENT TO CREDITORS:

Go Back To Your Monthly Expenses Worksheet

At the end of each month, take a few minutes to summarize and record all of your actual spending, including out-of-pocket spending, on the Monthly Expenses worksheet (pages 12 and 13).

On the bottom section of page 13, total all of your actual fixed, variable and periodic expenditures (listed in green boxes on pages 12 and 13) and subtract that figure from your Total Net Income for that month (listed in green box on page 4). This gives you your Excess Available for Debt Reduction. Next, enter your Total Monthly Payment to Creditors (listed above in green box) and subtract it from your Excess Available for Debt Reduction. The total is your Total Excess or Deficit.

Ideally, your budget will balance. Don't get discouraged if it doesn't on the first-month try. Review your list of Potential Reductions from your worksheet and put them into action.

It very well may take several months to get your budget to where everything falls into place. However, if you continue to look for more ways to spend less than your income, you will soon succeed. Good luck!

Commit To A Savings Plan

Saving, regularly setting aside part of your income, is an essential part of any money management plan.

Savings can provide the money we need to manage our regular financial obligations, meet our short-term and long-

term goals, plan for retirement and increase our financial security and family's sense of well-being.

Develop and commit to a savings plan that includes savings for regular living expenses, an emergency fund, short- and long-term goals and retirement.

Set Aside Savings For Periodic Living Expenses

Each pay period, set aside the amount that is budgeted for an expense but not actually spent during that pay period.

For example: Car maintenance budget amount $50.00
                 Car maintenance expenditures   −$30.00
                                                   $20.00 deposited into savings*

*Note: This should be an account such as a bank passbook savings account or interest-bearing checking account in which funds can be easily deposited and withdrawn, and should yield some interest. Funds in this account should be tracked; that way, you know how much is in the account and how those funds have been designated.

Saving For Short- And Long-Term Goals And Emergencies

Each pay period, set aside the amount that is budgeted for short- and long-term goals and an emergency fund. These funds can also be set aside in the same account as those for regular living expenses.

Once funds begin to grow, especially in the long-term goals category, you will need to move at least a portion of those funds into a savings instrument that will provide a higher rate of return.

For example, once savings for a long-term goal reach $500, that money can be put into a savings instrument such as a certificate of deposit (CD), which will earn higher interest than the savings account.

Questions that should be considered when evaluating a savings and investment instrument are:

- What is the interest rate?
- For how long must I invest the money?
- Can I have access to it at any time or is there a penalty if it is withdrawn early?
- Are there tax penalties if I withdraw the money early?
- Will my investment be risk-free?

Use the worksheet on the page 22 to keep track of your savings.

Saving For Retirement

Retirement savings should reflect your planned standard of living and should take your long-term healthcare needs into consideration. Income for retirement can include Social Security, pension and retirement funds such as individual retirement accounts (IRAs), and employer-sponsored plans, such as the 401(k) and 403(b).

Retirement savings and planning can best be addressed by consulting a certified financial planner.

Tip: A savings plan is essential to personal money management. Don't plan to save what is left over after all the bills are paid. Make saving a priority.

Tracking Your Savings Worksheet

Deposit/ Withdrawal Total	Emergency Fund	Long-Term Goals	Short-Term Goals	Car Repair/ Maintenance	Car Insurance/ License/Tax	Home Repair	Medical	Clothing	Balance
+100.00	25.00		5.00	20.00	5.00	5.00	20.00	20.00	100.00
+50.00	25.00	5.00						20.00	150.00
+75.00	25.00			20.00	5.00	25.00			225.00
Đ30.00				Đ20.00				Đ10.00	
TOTAL	75.00	5.00	5.00	20.00	10.00	30.00	20.00	30.00	195.00

Deposit/ Withdrawal Total	Emergency Fund	Long-Term Goals	Short-Term Goals	Car Repair/ Maintenance	Car Insurance/ License/Tax	Home Repair	Medical	Clothing	Balance

You've determined your budget, and you know how to get to where you want to be financially. To help assure success, ask everyone in your household to follow these rules of budgeting:

Communicate: Take the time to talk about each person's needs and wants so that all family members feel that they are a part of the plan.

Cooperate: Be prepared to compromise and work cooperatively. No one family member should be allowed to tell everyone else what they can or cannot spend. Instead, seek a financial partnership.

Control: Every family member must exercise control and avoid unnecessary spending. Once the budget plan is made, opportunities to overspend will occur daily. Each household member needs to encourage other family members to stick to the plan. Goods and services bought on impulse today become tomorrow's ghosts that haunt us in our closets, drawers, storage rooms and checking account balances.

Tip: Know when to get help. If your family's budgeting efforts don't bring the results you want, or if your debt seems overwhelming, consider seeking budget and debt counseling.

Do It!

CONSUMER DEBT COUNSELING®

and Consumer Credit Counseling Service-St. Louis

Help Is Only A Phone Call Away.

CDC Consumer Debt Counseling Inc. provides professional budget and debt management counseling. It operates offices in five states under the Consumer Debt Counseling and Consumer Credit Counseling Service-St. Louis names. The agency's certified counselors can help you work out solutions to your debt problems and gain control of your finances.

CDC is a nonprofit community service organization designed to help you help yourself get out of debt. For more information or to make an appointment with a counselor, please call us at:

Member of the National Foundation for Credit Counseling the Consumer Federation of America and the Better Business Bureau

Affiliated with the National Council on Economic Education and the Center for Entrepreneurship and Economic Education, University of Missouri-St. Louis

ACCREDITED

COUNCIL ON ACCREDITATION OF SERVICES FOR FAMILIES AND CHILDREN, INC.

1-800-9-NO-DEBT
(1-800-966-3328)

Main Office for CDC and CCCS-St. Louis:
1300 Hampton Avenue • St. Louis, MO 63139-8901

For additional copies, please call 1-800-966-3328, extension 1607.
Reprinted with permission of CDC Consumer Debt Counseling Inc.

Main Office:
1300 Hampton Avenue
St. Louis, MO 63139-8901
1-800-966-3328
www.consumerdebtcounseling.org
www.cccsstl.org

CONSUMER DEBT COUNSELING®

and Consumer Credit Counseling Service-St. Loui

male _____ female _____

age _____

 1. What one area impacted you the most?

 2. What one area impacted you the least?

 3. I found the information in this program to be ...
 circle one

very valuable   5   4   3   2   1   of little value.

 4. My understanding of marriage has ...
circle one

broadened   5   4   3   2   1   remained the same.

 5. I found that completing the exercises in the workbook was ...
circle one

helpful   5   4   3   2   1   not helpful.

 6. Please rate the following on a scale of 1-5, where 1 is awful and 5 is great.
 circle one

	Great				**Awful**
Icebreaker	5	4	3	2	1
Your facilitator couple	5	4	3	2	1
Facilitator experience story	5	4	3	2	1
Location of the class	5	4	3	2	1
The closing ceremony	5	4	3	2	1
The video	5	4	3	2	1

7. Check all that apply.

Am I glad I came to *Today and All the Days of Your Life*?

____Yes   ____ No

Would I recommend this program to a friend?

____Yes   ____ No

Do I more fully understand the vows and promises?

____Yes   ____No

Did I like the structure of this program?

____Yes   ____No

Did I have enough time to complete the questions in the book?

____Yes   ____No

Do I feel more prepared to commit to a sacramental marriage, now that I have completed the program?

____Yes   ____No

Will I complete this process by finishing any part of the workbook I wasn't able to complete in class and discuss the material with my fiancé?

____Yes   ____No

8. Is there anything you would like to tell your facilitator couple?

Love Letter

Our Collaborators are...

Video Production by:
Stepstone Productions, Inc.
Chuck Neff, Chairman/CEO
500 S. Ewing
Saint Louis, MO 63103
314.436.4449
www.stepstoneproductions.org

Cover Art Design by:
Roadhat Multimedia Production Co.
R.T. Radanovich, Producer
500 S. Ewing, Suite F
Saint Louis, MO 63103
314.504.5122
RT@Roadhat.com

DTR Communication Skill:
The PAIRS Foundation
(Practical Application of Intimate
Relationship Skills)
1.888.485.7080
www.PAIRS.com

Family Planning/Fertility Care Information:
The Department of Natural Family Planning
K. Diane Daly, R.N.
11700 Studt Avenue, Suite c
Saint Louis, MO 63141
314.997.7576 ext.254
dalydk@stlo.smhs.com

The Newlyweds' Guide to Money Management
Consumer Debt Counseling
Victoria Jacobson, M.Ed., President
The Foundation for Credit Education
1300 Hampton Avenue
Saint Louis, MO 63139
314.647.9004
www.foundationforcrediteducation.org

Workbook and Facilitator Guide Design and Layout:
Erin Convy
Graphic Designer
314.725.8478
econvy@prodigy.net